CLASSICAL GARDENS
IN CHINA

TITLES IN THE SERIES

Chinese Ceramics
JI WEI

Chinese Characters
NINA TRAIN CHOA

Chinese Calligraphy
ZHOU KEXI

Chinese Painting
DENG MING

Chinese Tea
LING YUN

50 Amazing Places in China
DONG HUAI

56 Ethnic Groups in China
DAI DUNBANG

Famous Flowers in China
QIAN XINGJIAN

Chinese Motifs of Good Fortune
LIU SHENGHUI & ZHU WEN

Chinese Architecture
WANG QIJUN

Contemporary Architecture in China
ARCHITECTURAL CREATION MAGAZINE

The Giant Panda
FANG MIN

Classical Gardens in China
LIU TUO

Bamboo in China
SHEN MIN

Discovering China

CLASSICAL GARDENS IN CHINA

BY LIU TUO

Better Link Press

This book is edited and designed by the Editorial Committee of *Cultural China* series

Managing Directors: Wang Youbu, Xu Naiqing

Editorial Director: Wu Ying

Editors: Yang Xiaohe, Susan Luu Xiang

Text by Liu Tuo

Photographs and Illustrations Provided by Liu Tuo

Translation by Qiu Maoru

Cover Design: Wang Wei

Interior Design: Yuan Yinchang, Li Jing, Hu Bin

Cover Image: Quanjing

ISBN: 978-1-60220-131-6

Address any comments about *Discovering China: Classical Gardens in China* to:

Better Link Press

99 Park Ave

New York, NY 10016

USA

or

Shanghai Press and Publishing Development Company

F 7 Donghu Road, Shanghai, China (200031)

Email: comments_betterlinkpress@hotmail.com

Printed in China by Shenzhen Donnelley Printing Co., Ltd.

1   3   5   7   9   10   8   6   4   2

CONTENTS

CONTENTS

PREFACE

Garden building is not only an ancient art, but also an innovative art. Highly developed human society makes people live a social life farther and farther away from natural surroundings. In fact, Mother Nature endows humankind, as part of nature, with a natural attribute. With the constant sophistication of their living environment, people conceive an earnest desire to return to nature. In spite of their ethnic and regional diversity, all the countries in the world have their own garden cultures as long as their economy and culture have reached a certain stage of development. Age-long historical development, inheritances from generation to generation and mutual influence combine to bring about the brilliant culture of classical gardens. The further growth of modern society has witnessed a new trend of modern garden art: on the one hand a group of national parks and natural resorts based on natural scenery have come into being; on the other hand artificial gardens have been built as parks at intersections, community parks and residential gardens—all close to people's life. No matter in which way the garden art is developed, classical gardens are the foundation of modern gardens and the origin of garden art. As an embodiment of cultural achievements of humankind, classical gardens serve as the source of the present-day creative garden art. Drawing from the inexhaustible intellectual wealth of classical gardens, people take advantage of those best and convenient "natural spaces" to refine their thoughts, change their moods and relax themselves.

The design of a garden is itself a comprehensive creative art involving garden engineering, construction, horticulture, sculpture, mural painting and calligraphy. While enjoying the beauty of garden art, one is imbued with a fine artistic taste of various forms of art and regards it as an aesthetic treat.

CHAPTER 1

LONG-STANDING ART

China's garden art has a very long history. Full of cultural symbols and distinct styles, it is one of the most represented art forms of traditional Chinese culture.

China's classical gardens can be traced back to the "animal farm" in the Shang (c.1600 – 1046 BC) and Zhou (c.1046 – 256 BC) dynasties. The "animal farm", with a natural landscape of hills and streams, was more like a game reserve where fodders were grown and animals were bred for the pleasure of hunting by the emperors. An "animal farm" covered a large area. As noted in *The Book of Songs*, the animal farm of Emperor Wen of the Zhou dynasty extended as far as 70 *li* (1 *li* equals 0.31 miles). There were magnificent earth terraces, big ponds filled with a great variety of fishes and forested hills scattered with reared animals, mainly deer and birds. Because people did not free themselves from the mentality of depending on nature, the "animal farm" was not seen as a creative art form. However, the Spring and Autumn period (770 – 476 BC) and the Warring States period (475 – 221 BC) witnessed the thriving development of garden designing and building that transformed the primitive status of the "animal farm" and ushered in the era of the man-made garden.

In 505 BC Fu Chai, King of Wu Kingdom, gave orders to build a huge garden called "Gu Su Tai" (which literally means "Suzhou Terrace") for Xi Shi—one of the four famous beauties in Chinese history—on the Gusu Hill which was situated 8 miles away to the southwest of Suzhou. It is recorded that Gu Su Tai's main terrace, which was 26 meters long and 100 meters high, commanded an extensive view of 300 *li*. The winding corridors and verandas attached to the terrace were as long as 5 *li*. Five

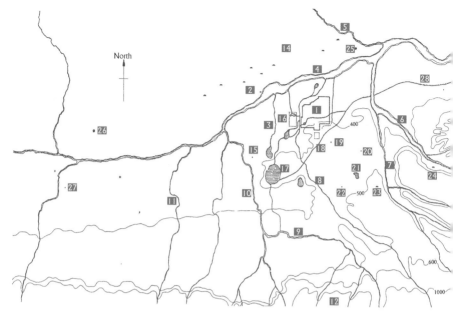

A Map of Palace Gardens during the Han Dynasty

The Shang Lin Yuan (Upper Forest Palace Garden) of the Han dynasty was rebuilt on the ruins of the Shang Lin Yuan of the Qin dynasty. The huge garden extended across five counties, including Chang'an and Xianning and was about 400 *li* in circumference. There were 10 natural lakes in the garden and the eight rivers of central Shaanxi flowed through the garden. It was known for as many as 3,000 different kinds of rare flowers and plants and several hundred species of precious birds and animals. Over 70 imperial palaces and residences were built in the garden. Taoist temples, pavilions and terraces were scattered about.

1. Chang'an 2. Xianyang 3. Hao River 4. Wei River 5. Jing River 6. Ba River 7. Chan River 8. Xue River 9. Jiao River 10. Feng River 11. Lao River 12. Zhongnan Mountain 13. Li Mountain 14. Imperial Mausoleum 15. Xuanqu Palace 16. Jianzhang Palace 17. Kunming Lake 18. Kunming Canal 19. Bowang Garden 20. Leyou Garden 21. Yichun Garden 22. Yusu Garden 23. Du Tomb 24. Ba Tomb 25. Lanchi Palace 26. Huangshan Palace 27. Changyang Palace, Wuzha Palace 28. Canal 29. Dinghu Palace

years' worth of state revenue was expended on the construction of this huge garden.

During the Qin (221 – 206 BC) and Han (206 BC – 220 AD) dynasties the man-made garden was a common presence in both imperial and private residences. The large scope, great number and beautiful scenery of gardens were unprecedented in China's garden-building history. The garden designers made a breakthrough in depicting the symbols and themes of the garden layout and internal scenes, which was later seen as

Pond Seen in the Stone Relief of the Han Dynasty

The Jianzhang Palace was one of the most important palace gardens built in the Shang Lin Yuan. The man-made Taiye Pond was decorated with three islands symbolizing the three fabled mountains (Yingzhou, Penglai and Fangzhang) of immortals. Plants like the wild rice were grown around the pond while aquatic plants such as lotus and water caltrops were cultivated inside the pond. Groups of pelicans, partridges, purple tortoises and green turtles frolicked about on the shore of the pond. Small boats made out of crab apple trees sailed swiftly on the water.

the forerunner of the forthcoming theme parks. The early representative gardens of this kind were "Shang Lin Yuan (Upper Forest Palace Garden)" and "E Pang Gong (Epang Garden Palace)" built in Xianyang, the capital of the Qin dynasty. Situated in Xianyang during the Qin dynasty, the Shang Lin Yuan was an architectural complex of garden palaces, which covered a huge area, and the famous E Pang Garden Palace was one of them.

Based on scenic palace gardens of the Qin dynasty, the garden

Garden Seen in the Stone Relief of the Han Dynasty

As described in the book *Notes about Chang'an*, Yuan Guanghan, a man of wealth in Maoling, had a private garden called "Beimang Mountain Garden" that was 5 *li* long from north to south and 4 *li* wide from east to west. A man-made pond was filled with water transported from elsewhere. The 40 meter high artificial hill extended several *li*. The garden was flushed with rare and precious birds, trees and plants. Elegant houses, pavilions and winding corridors were clustered all around.

building of the Han dynasty was further developed to artificially imitate and sometimes even create natural scenery. The much larger Shang Lin Yuan of the Han dynasty was typical of imperial gardens at that time. In addition to imperial gardens, there was a dynamic growth of private gardens. For example, the Liang Yuan (Liang Garden) was famous for a harmonious combination of beautiful hills, ponds, flowers and trees complemented by eye-catching buildings and colorful human activities of cultural significance.

With the spread of Taoism, garden art incorporated the building of mystical lands into its designs. With this conception put into practice, garden designers built the novel landscape of offshore mountains inhabited by immortals and a mystical land on the Penglai Island. Three imitated mountains of immortals were built in the big man-made pond to symbolize respectively the three fabled abodes of immortals, i.e., Penglai, Fangzhang and Yingzhou.

The gardens built during the Qin and Han dynasties were featured by the early realistic style of artificially imitating natural scenery. Natural

Copy of *Painting of Wangchuan Villa* of the Tang Dynasty

Wang Wei (701 – 761), poet and painter of the Tang dynasty, created in his Wangchuan Villa more than 20 scenes including Mengcheng Col, Huazi Ridge, Wenxing Mansion and Jinzhu Mountain. The painter used scenes to express his feelings so that every scene had an implied meaning. Wang Wei formulated a style of his own and attained a high degree of perfection in designing scenes in his painting, composing poems based on scenes and incorporating poems into his paintings. Acting the role of garden designer, poet and painter at the same time, Wang Wei applied his artistic conception of incorporating poetry and painting into garden designing, thus achieving a remarkable feat unprecedented before the Tang dynasty.

hills and streams were copied and reproduced in garden building on a large scale and in a supernatural way. However, the imitation focused on their form only and little heed was paid to exploring the spiritual function of man-made gardens. As a branch of art, gardens of that historical period were lacking in the exploration of their deep connotations, the representation of their spirit or in the pursuit of their artistic conception.

During the war-ridden years of Wei (220 – 265), Jin (265 – 420) and the Northern and Southern dynasties (420 – 589) people lived a dissipated life and decadent customs were becoming increasingly widespread. Both the ruling class and intellectuals tried to escape reality by indulging in pleasures of enjoying beautiful gardens. Garden landscape was not only a visual feast, but also a material instrument to convey the garden owner's feelings and emotion. The Jin Gu Yuan (Jin'gu Garden) owned by Shi Chong of the Western Jin dynasty was typical of the early works of garden art in that historical period.

The Eastern Jin dynasty saw the appearance of spirit-catching trend in garden designing. Interaction between viewers and scenes made their roles interchangeable from time to time. The narrow scope of a scenic environment or the simplicity of scenes was surmounted when designers began to focus on the garden's function instead of its vastness or spaciousness. This new trend can be best reflected by the following sayings: "one can find a cozy nest even on a branch" and "one can express his full emotion and feelings even at the sight of a tiny pebble or a single bamboo."

Another special phenomenon in garden design and building worth mentioning during the Wei and Jin dynasties was the emergence of a large number of temple-attached gardens influenced by the quick spread of Buddhism and Taoism during those turbulent years. The temple-attached gardens were grouped into three categories. The surrounding mountains administered by temples belonged to the first category—exterior gardens. They included Mount Tai (in Shandong Province), Mount Hua (in Shaanxi Province), Mount Heng (in Shanxi Province), Mount Heng (in Hunan Province), Mount Song (in Henan Province), Mount E'mei (in Sichuan Province), Mount Wutai (in Shanxi Province), Mount Jiuhua (in Anhui Province) and Mount Putuo (in Zhejiang Province). Interior gardens belonged to the second category, with the Jin Ci (Jin Ancestral Temple) being a typical example of this in a later period. The independent gardens built either inside the temple or by the side of the temple fell under the third category. Gardens of this type were often called "western gardens" to signify the Western Paradise advocated by Buddhism. These three different types of gardens shared a common feature, i.e., to attach importance to their spiritual aesthetic function so as to be free from worldly vulgarity.

Copy of *A Prize Contest Held in Jinming Pond*

During the Tang and Song dynasties a mature conception of garden building brought about a renewed and enriched content to gardens. For example, sports and amusement facilities were incorporated into the designing of palace gardens. The most popular ones were polo fields, ball-kicking courses and spa bath ponds. The *A Prize Contest Held in Jinming Pond* depicted the emperor, accompanied by his favorite ministers, watching the water fight and dragon-boat race held in the pond.

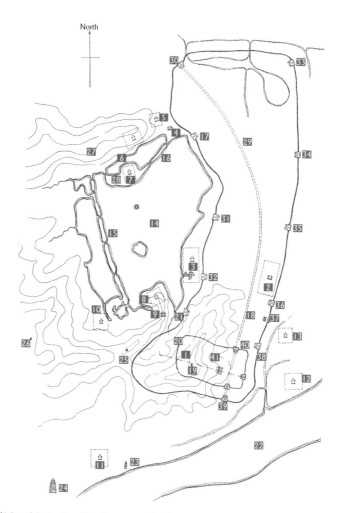

North

A Map of Lin'an of the Southern Song Dynasty and the Plan of the West Lake and Major Palace Gardens

The characteristics and functions of gardens underwent a drastic change in the Tang and Song dynasties. The gardens similar to modern urban parks were developed during that period. The West Lake in Lin'an (present-day Hangzhou) of the Southern Song dynasty became a tourist attraction for officials, gentry, scholars and common people alike. There, they enjoyed the cool weather and admired beautiful flowers, went boating and climbed hills and attended acrobatic performances and evening parties with singing and dancing.

Major palace gardens:

1. Imperial Garden 2. Deshou Palace 3. Jujing Garden 4. Zhaoqing Temple 5. Yuhu Garden 6. Jifang Garden 7. Yanxiang Garden 8. Pingshan Garden 9. Jingci Temple 10. Qingle Garden 11. Yujin Garden 12. Fujing Garden 13. Wuliu Garden 14. West Lake 15. Su Causeway 16. Bai Causeway 17. Qiantang Gate 18. District of Government Offices 19. Fenghuang Mountain 20. Wansong Mountain 21. Long Bridge 22. Qiantang River 23. White Pagoda 24. Liuhe Pagoda 25. Nanping Mountain 26. Southern Peak 27. Ge Mountain 28. Gu Mountain 29. Imperial Road 30. Yuhang Gate 31. Yongjin Gate 32. Qingbo Gate 33. Genshan Gate 34. Dongqing Gate 35. Chongxin Gate 36. Xin Gate 37. Bao'an Gate 38. Houchao Gate 39. Jiahui Gate 40. Hening Gate 41. Palace City

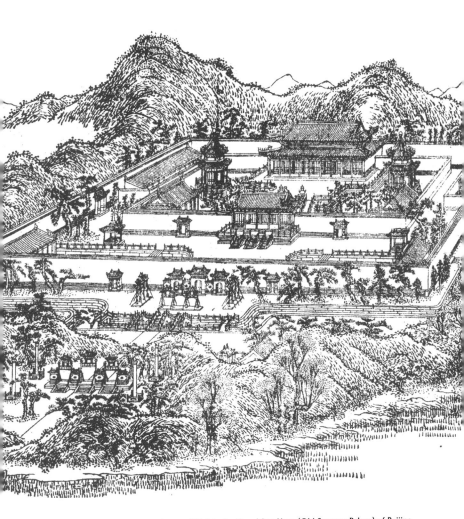

A Bird's-eye View of Hongci-yonggu Ancestral Hall in the Yuan Ming Yuan (Old Summer Palace) of Beijing

In the year 1742 Emperor Qianlong of the Qing dynasty spent 600,000 taels of silver building the Hongci-yonggu Ancestral Hall in the Yuan Ming Yuan. Its principal building, Anyou Palace, was situated in the center at the end of a mountain path with a southern exposure. Its building materials consisted mainly of stones and marbles. Quite a distance away from its gate stood two pair of ornamental columns in front of the memorial arch. Topped by light yellow glazed tiles and eaves, the columns were guarded by 4 marble railings, a stone beast and several pillars carved with dragons, clouds and flames.

A Bird's-eye View of the Wang Shi Yuan (Master of the Nets Garden) in Suzhou

The Wang Shi Yuan was a masterpiece of small and medium-sized classical gardens in the south of the Yangtze River. It was known for its crafty planning, compact layout, refined architecture and harmonious spatial proportion. The garden was composed of three sections with different ambience. The east section was the residential quarters while the middle section was the main garden. The pond of the main garden was built with yellow stones whereas other courtyards were decorated with Taihu rocks. The water-centered landscape was surrounded by properly spaced pavilions and quiet and tasteful winding corridors. A poetic mood would come over everyone who visited this beautiful garden.

The Tang (618 – 907) and Song (960 – 1279) dynasties saw another cumulation of rapid development in the art of China's classical gardens. During Zhenguan and Yonghui era of the Tang dynasty, the rulers exerted themselves to make their country strong and vigorous. More and more palace gardens were built: the Xi Nei Yuan (West Palace Garden), Dong Nei Yuan (East Palace Garden), Jing Yuan (Forbidden Garden) and Furong Yuan (Hibiscus Garden) were built in Chang'an (present-day Xi'an, Shaanxi Province). Such beautiful gardens as the Yuhua Palace, Xianyou Palace, Huaqing Palace and Jiucheng Palace were scattered on the outskirts. Of the palace gardens built by emperors of the Song dynasty the most well known was the Shou Shan Gen Yue (Shou Mountain and Gen Mountain). For the purpose of building it, a great variety of rare and precious flowers, plants, bamboos and rocks of south China were requisitioned and transported to Bianjing (present-day Kaifeng, Henan Province). This drained the treasury and exhausted the labor in such a way that incurred the wrath of the people and prompted them into rebellion.

The garden designing of the Song dynasty was distinguished by the division of scenic zones in a garden with different themes and characteristics. This conception of the Song designers' fully demonstrated their artistic pursuit in recreating the essence of nature.

The scholars of the Tang and Song dynasties firmly advocated the spiritual and social functions of gardens and determined these to be the substances of garden art. During the Tang and Song dynasties, people visited gardens for the purpose of emotional refinement and meditation.

The aesthetic taste and standards of gardens were gradually perfected through large-scale and high-class practice of garden design and building. The gardens favored by scholars were distinguished by their

A Shoal of Fish in the Tui Si Yuan (Retreat & Reflection Garden) of Tongli

In addition to hills, ponds, flowers, trees and buildings, animals are also a key element of China's gardens. The most frequently seen animals in gardens are deer, cranes, tortoises, fish and aquatic birds.

literary flavor, including design conception, theme expansion, scene materials and implication, styles of inscriptions and calligraphy, etc. The scholars of that historical period tended to incorporate their feelings and emotion, especially the sentiment and moral integrity of feudal scholars, into the design of gardens.

As bamboo symbolized elegant and refined manners, the famous poet Su Shi (1037 – 1101) wrote this poem: "While one can live without meat, one can't live without bamboo. A meal without meat makes one thin whereas a life without bamboo makes one vulgar." In China's gardens meaningful plants included the pine, plum, chrysanthemum, osmanthus, beech, parasol, ginkgo, lotus, day lily, to name but a few.

While the influence of living a practical life still remained, people began to harbor a desire to lead an imaginary life in the Song dynasty. Compared with the heyday of the Tang dynasty, the national power of the Song dynasty was declining. Social upheavals cast a shadow on the mind of scholars and scholar-officials. As a result they went in for garden building in a big way. They found themselves a cozy nest in their gardens where they took advantage of the scenery to express their feelings, thus mitigating their sorrows and attaining mental balance.

The garden art was further developed during the Ming (1368 –

The Yi Pu (Garden of Arts) of Suzhou

The scholars' gardens in the south of the Yangtze River resemble a fresh and tasteful Chinese ink-and-wash painting. They are usually long and narrow, enclosed by grey-tiled whitewashed walls and decorated with exquisite rockeries, beautiful flowers and green plants.

1644) and Qing (1644 – 1911) dynasties. Starting from the Ming dynasty, the change of social structure and the growth of a commodity economy promoted the thriving development of garden art. On the one hand, many artistically refined gardens revealed a target-oriented trend toward stylization. On the other hand, an emphasis was put on the practical value of gardens as a necessary environment for daily life popularized garden art. After thousands of years' practice and tempering China's garden art reached perfection during the Ming and Qing dynasties. With the conception gradually enlarged and garden-building technology meticulously advanced, the garden designers and builders of that historical period created and handed down a great many elegant and refined masterpieces of garden art. Among them are the famous imperial gardens, including the Yuan Ming Yuan (Old Summer Palace), the Yi He Yuan (Summer Palace) in Beijing, the Bi Shu Shan Zhuang (Chengde Mountain Resort) in Chengde. Well-known private gardens were the Zhuo Zheng Yuan (Humble Administrator's Garden), the Wang Shi Yuan (Master of the Nets Garden), the Liu Yuan (Lingering Garden), the Cang Lang Ting (Blue Waves Pavilion) and the Shi Zi Lin (Lion Grove) in Suzhou, the Xiao Pan Gu (Xiaopangu Garden), Ge Yuan (Individual or Isolated Garden), the He Yuan (He Garden) and the Pian Shi Shan Fang (Silver of Rock Mountain Cottage) in Yangzhou, the Ji Chang Yuan (Garden of Lodging One's Expansive Feelings) in Wuxi, the Tui Si Yuan (Retreat & Reflection Garden) in Wujiang, the Yu Yuan (Garden to Please), the Qiu Xia Pu (Garden of Autumn Vapours) and the Gu Yi Yuan (Ancient Garden of Elegance) in Shanghai, the Sui Yuan, the Zhan Yuan (Outlook Garden) and the Xu Yuan (Warm Garden) in Nanjing, and many other tastefully laid-out gardens in the areas south of the Yangtze River and in southern China.

CHAPTER 2
NATURE-LIKE LANDSCAPE

In the 18th century an Italian missionary gave a first-hand account of the differences in landscape between Chinese and European gardens: "The gardens in Europe pursue the artistic perfection at the sacrifice of nature. The European garden builders level the ground by removing hills, drying up lakes and felling trees. They prefer to pave a straight path, construct fountains and plant row upon row of flowers. On the contrary, the Chinese garden builders imitate nature in an artistic way. That's why their gardens are known for varied topography including artificial hills reached by sometimes straight and sometimes zigzag paths. Some paths cross level land, some others pass through gullies and still some others traverse bridges. One may have to climb up unprocessed rocks to reach the top of a hill. The lake is scattered with islets on which stands a small temple only accessible by boat or bridge."

China's classical gardens advocate nature, pursue nature and reproduce nature. The essence of Chinese garden designing lies in revealing the inner beauty of natural form instead of imitating the outer beauty. This kind of inner beauty is exactly the "nature" depicted in the Taoist concept of "letting things take their own course" advocated by Laozi (also translated as Lao-tzu) and Zhuangzi (also translated as Chuang-tzu). That's the very reason why in Chinese garden designing special attention is paid to the borrowing of scenery, arrangement from top to bottom, compliance with physical features of a place and the removal of traces of man-made embellishment.

In ancient China people of upper and middle class social strata were

The Scenic Spot "Natural Portrayal" in the Yuan Ming Yuan (Old Summer Palace)

The distinguishing feature of China's classical gardens is their "naturalness." This conclusion was reached by a meticulous comparison in landscape between Chinese and European gardens. To be more exact, "naturalness" was the artistic goal and perfection the ancient Chinese set for themselves. From the Han and Tang dynasties to the Ming and Qing dynasties books about the history of garden building in China were full of expressions like "the exact copy of nature," "so wonderful about its naturalness," "just as if it is springing from nature" and "just like nature itself."

The Scenic Spot "True Meaning of the Lake and Hill" of the Yi He Yuan (Summer Palace)

In the Yi He Yuan there is an inscription with four Chinese characters: Hu Shan Zhen Yi, which means "the true meaning of the lake and hill." Even though the garden is man-made, the essence of the natural lake and hill is well kept. That conforms to the goal of Chinese garden building—"Though man-made, the garden looks as if it is springing from nature."

divided into two dwelling modes—house dwelling and garden dwelling. The inhabitants of a house usually led a dull and restrained life while those of a garden lived a leisurely and carefree life. Just as Wang Shizhen (1526 – 1590) of the Ming dynasty said, "solitary mountain dwelling and noisy downtown dwelling do not bear comparison with the ideal garden dwelling." His statement well illustrates a symbolic meaning, i.e., people tend to reflect upon and examine their thoughts and conduct so as to strike a balance between a social trend and a natural process, and what's more, between their natural character and social character.

As a special genre of art, China's classical gardens seem to be the imitation and extraction of nature on the surface, but are in essence the exploration of the way of the world. In pursuit of such a great goal, the ancient scholars and scholar-officials were able to experience the natural beauty of the landscape dotted with bright clouds, blue sky, clear water, green grassland, weeping willows, singing birds, etc. They sensed the harmony between themselves and nature, thus enjoying inward pleasure which surpassed the pursuit of fame and wealth.

Ji Cheng (1582 – 1642), a famous garden designer of the Ming dynasty, defined the essence of Chinese garden building as "Though man-made, the garden looks like it is springing from nature." His definition fully demonstrates that garden building is a creative process based on the high-degree extraction and artistic generalization of nature.

CHAPTER 3

DEEP IMPLICATIONS

J ust like writing poems and painting, the garden designers in ancient China would first determine a theme for the garden. While a general theme and conception was essential for the garden, different themes should be prepared for various scenic spots in the garden.

In addition to the apparent labeled themes, the subtle beauty of artistic ambience is the highest pursuit of the designers of China's classical gardens. In those gardens each special scenic spot indicates the designer's distinctive pursuit. It is very common in Chinese garden designing that every hill, every pond, every plant or every tree has a profound implication and is thought provoking. Chinese garden art attributes its colorful themes and subtle ambience to the original aesthetic thought on garden building and the extensive traditional Chinese culture. The thematic ideas are in support of the inner essence of gardens originate from the Confucian teaching of balanced poetic and rational education and the Taoist teaching of the belief in deities. In the meantime, Zen Buddhism makes a notable impact on Chinese garden art.

The Confucian teaching of balanced poetic and rational education. One important topic of Chinese classical philosophy is to study the relationship between natural phenomena and human affairs. In the traditional Confucian philosophy the relationship is described as "the theory that man is an integral part of nature" aiming at establishing harmony between three forces—man, heaven and earth. The three forces can merge into one by mutual participation. In Chinese garden building emphasis is laid on sentiment contained in scenery, sentiment mingled with scenery, message contained in scenes and truth revealed

Autumn Hill of the Ge Yuan (Individual or Isolated Garden) in Yangzhou

The artificial hills in the Ge Yuan of Yangzhou are named after the four seasons. Each hill is designed according to the theme of a particular season. The Autumn Hill is built by piling up yellow rocks to display the physique and color of autumn. The whole hill is covered with trees which leaves turn a fiery red in autumn.

Tingyu Chamber of the Zhuo Zheng Yuan (Humble Administrator's Garden) in Suzhou

The Tingyu (which means "listen to the rain") Chamber in the Zhuo Zheng Yuan is an independent courtyard in the garden. The horizontal board on the door lintel of the main structure is inscribed with three characters: "Ting Yu Xuan." In a quiet and secluded courtyard where there is a pond of limpid water, the careful observer will be able unveil the mystery of "listening to the rain" as it beats against the thick growth of green palm leaves.

by scenes. This is the embodiment of the Confucian thought on harmonious combination of inner and outer elements and that of subjective and objective elements. People regard natural scenes as the target for appreciation because they symbolize moral beauty, spiritual beauty and personality beauty. The color, lines, shape and proportion that are characteristic of natural beauty usually occupy a minor position in their aesthetic conception. People tend to experience from the symbolic meanings of natural scenes the harmony and unity between scenes and me, objective and subjective elements, inner and outer elements and between man and nature.

The Taoist teaching of belief in deities. Unlike religious ideology, the locally born and bred belief in deities presented to the ancient Chinese a "beautiful" future both within sight and within reach. Their dream was transformed into the scenes of gardens that constituted the greater part of the landscape in classical gardens of various dynasties. The First Emperor of the Qin dynasty built a man-made pond by drawing water from the Wei River and then put up the imitated Penglai Mountain in it. Emperor Wu of Han dynasty dug the Taiye Pond and put up such artificial mountains of immortals as Penglai, Fangzhang, Huliang and Yingzhou. Ever since then it became a common practice for people to dig ponds in their gardens and build artificial mountains of immortals there. The designing of China's classical gardens in

A Bird's-eye View of the Wonder Terrace of the Peng Island in the Yuan Ming Yuan (Old Summer Palace)

Because the general public was fond of the idea of heaven and paradise, the garden designers incorprated aspects of these things in their landscaping, such as marble towers, jade halls, fairy ponds and leisure terraces. Some designers even raised deer and cranes in the garden to imitate the carefree life of immortals.

The Zhiyu Bridge in the Xiequ Garden of the Yi He Yuan (Summer Palace) in Beijing

The landscape of the Xiequ Garden is fill with poetic beauty. Upon entering, you will come across various inscription boards with couplets describing the scene in front of you. A winding corridor is simply named "Poem-hunting Path", enticing visitors to look for poems that they will find it difficult to tear themselves away from the tiny space.

The Yiliang Pavilion in the Zhuo Zheng Yuan (Humble Administrator's Garden) of Suzhou

The inscriptions of China's classical gardens are mostly quoted directly or adapted from the poems of predecessors. Take the Yiliang (literally means "dual suitability") Pavilion for example. It is adapted from Bai Juyi's poem "A green poplar ushers in spring for both families." As this pavilion forms a natural boundary between the middle and western sections of the Zhuo Zheng Yuan, it commands a good view of the scenes in both sections.

The Scenic Spot "The Tour of a Painting" in the Yi He Yuan (Summer Palace) of Beijing

Another distinguishing feature of Chinese garden art is to draw inspiration from paintings and reproduce the picturesque scenes in the garden landscape. Half way up the western side of the Longevity Hill in the Yi He Yuan there is a scenic spot called "The Tour of a Painting." This area is scattered with evenly spaced pavilions and artistically piled rocks, giving visitors the sense of being part of a painting.

this way originated from the designers' intention of reproducing natural scenes. However, it also represented ancient Chinese people's concept of an ideal secular life. However naïve, vain, vulgar or aloof they might be, they shared, in various degrees, a eulogy to life and the pursuit of an ideal future. Their pursuit in turn developed the technology of garden building and greatly enriched the connotation and expression of the garden landscape.

Zen Buddhism. Zen Buddhism did not influence directly the sign language of garden landscape because it was opposed to the inexhaustibility and credibility of language expression. It made a great impact on the personality of Chinese scholars and scholar-officials and their aesthetic standards, thus changing their aesthetic taste of garden styles and landscaping. According to the teaching of Zen Buddhism, the dharma-realm is universal. The difference of all the things in the universe depends on the change of the Buddhist law or one's original intention. Everything that is possessed by a high mountain or a large river can also found in a single plant or a tiny stone, and vice versa. It is true to say that "green bamboos are the body of Buddha whereas yellow flowers are the highest wisdom." This theory leaves little room to doubt the possibility of the unlimited appreciation of the limited garden landscape, thus removing a line of demarcation between small nature

Borrowing Scenes in the Yi He Yuan (Summer Palace) of Beijing

The eastern shore of the South Lake in the Summer Palace of Beijing is the best place to enjoy the beautiful scenes of the front mountain and the front lake. In addition to the wooded Longevity Hill and mist-covered Kunming Lake, the borrowed scenes of the graceful shape of the Yuquan Hill and the towering peak of the Western Hills come into view. The well-spaced and well-proportioned landscape demonstrates that the scenes in the garden and the borrowed scenes are in perfect harmony and form an integral whole.

The Contrasting Scene in the Zhuo Zheng Yuan (Humble Administrator's Garden) of Suzhou

The unexpected contrasting scenes are the most ideal. One of the best examples of these scenes is in the Loquat Garden of the Zhuo Zheng Yuan. When a visitor passes through the "Sunset Green" archway, he will catch sight of something out of a landscape painting–the Xuexiang-yunwei Pavilion standing luminously among a grove of green trees.

and big nature. This provides a theoretical basis for scholars to experience big nature through the appreciation of the small nature of garden landscape. The artistic ambience of China's classical gardens and that of traditional Chinese poetry and landscape paintings are interlinked. Every scene in the garden is itself a beautiful painting and serves as source material for creating paintings and poems. In other words, the garden art is itself a three-dimensional painting and a still poem. That is why people always compare the artistic ambience of garden landscape to poetic beauty or picturesque scenery.

The picturesque landscape of a classical garden is achieved by means of borrowing, contrasting and adorning the scenery. To contrast the scenery means to make every scene the place and target of observation. As a result visitors feel like they are part of the scenery. To borrow the scenery means to make the outside scenery a component part of the garden landscape or to make scenes in the garden complement each other. In this way the gradation of the garden landscape will be enhanced and space perception will be increased. In addition to borrowing and contrasting the scenery, to adorn the scenery is also a common landscaping technique. Take the Wang Shi Yuan (Master of the Nets Garden) for example. There was a white wall on the eastern shore of its pond. The garden builder cleverly piled up some yellow stones and planted some sparsely spaced green trees, thus turning the dull wall into a quiet but tasteful painting.

CHAPTER 4

VARIED SPACES

The most important artistic character of China's classical gardens is the sense of space. One is required to place oneself within a space before he can enjoy and experience the beauty of the garden landscape. This characteristic is manifested by one's feeling of viewing all nature by observing a tiny scene in the garden. It seems to a visitor that a big forest is nearby, the winding path is without end and the change of contrasting scenes is endless. In a word, the garden designers try their best to awaken a visitor's imagination so as to turn the limited space he sees into infinite dreamland. In order to produce such an artistic effect, the garden designers usually divide the whole garden into several scenes or landscape units to prevent visitors from taking in the whole landscape at a glance lest they find the tour dull and boring. The garden designers adopt various camouflage approaches to make each scene independent and bring about a variation of space. Camouflage barriers are divided into two kinds—solid ones and nominal ones. The former are blocking barriers such as a rockery or a building. They are meant to separate different scenes instead of surrounding a scene. The latter include pane-free windows, open corridors, flowers and other plants. Take the Xiaocanglang Pavilion in the Zhuo Zheng Yuan (Humble Administrator's Garden) for example. The covered bridge is used as a camouflage barrier to block the northern view. Its scanty and light structure looks like a half barrier, which, instead of blocking completely a visitor's sight, serves to add the gradation of the garden landscape.

To conform to the different artistic ambience and theme of each scene in the garden, a great variety of spatial forms are adopted and arranged. For example, before you enter a fairly spacious scenic spot, you are often

A Bird's-eye View of the Jiajing-mingqin Scenic Spot of the Old Summer Palace of Beijing

The useful part of a jug or a house is not its wall, but its inner "nothingness," i.e., space. For the same reason, the greatest artistic value a garden posseses is its space. The garden space is an environment of special flavor composed of hills, ponds, flowers, plants and buildings. Visitors will be impressed by its solemnity, brightness, cordiality, gracefulness, serenity, melancholy and mystery.

compelled to go through a dark, narrow and zigzag space. In this way your eyesight is restrained. Then all of a sudden, you will be surprised to find yourself in a bright open space. As a common practice, a winding corridor or a small courtyard is built next to the gate of a garden to serve as a foil for the principal scenes of the garden. For example, when you enter the side door of the Zhuo Zheng Yuan, you have to pass through two half-enclosed spaces before you come to the main garden. After you enter the gate of the East Palace of the Summer Palace, you have to go through the orderly arranged and enclosed imperial courtyards of the Renshou Palace and the Leshou Hall before you feast your eyes on a much broader view

The Winding Corridors of the Gardens in Suzhou

The purposeful design of the narrow paths and winding corridors is to empathize the deep and secluded space of the garden. The extended path also serves to prolong your tour and gives you the impression that the small scenes don't look too small and the close-up scenes don't look too close.

The Xiaocanglang Pavilion in the Zhuo Zheng Yuan (Humble Administrator's Garden) of Suzhou

The covered bridge is used as a camouflage barrier to block the northern view. Its low structure is a half barrier that, instead of blocking a visitor's sight completely, serves to add to the gradation of the garden landscape.

The Bamboo Sequestered Residence in the Humble Administrator's Garden of Suzhou

On one side of the Humble Administrator's Garden are composed of several groups of independent small-space scenes, such as the Bamboo Sequestered Residence, the Flowering Crabapple Terrace, the Loquat Garden and the Listening-to-the-Rain Chamber. These independent small-space scenes with spring rain or autumn fruit as their themes, or flowering crabapples or Chinese parasol trees as their views, are in such marked contrast to the big-space landscape of the main garden that they offer visitors a great artistic treat.

of the front hill and the front lake. The approach of "being restrained for the purpose of showcasing the more beautiful" is also adopted in the landscaping of the Jingxin Study of the Bei Hai Gong Yuan (Beihai Park), the Wang Shi Yuan (Master of the Nets Garden), the Liu Yuan (Lingering Garden) and the Shi Zi Lin (Lion Grove) of Suzhou.

Another common technique of garden space designing is to put a smaller space within or beside a bigger space, thus creating "a garden within a garden." The contrast in size makes the garden rich in spatial structure.

Besides the art of space arrangement, China's classical gardens are an art of time arrangement. A tour of a garden is a process of continuous sightseeing for a visitor. But a garden designer has to factor time into consideration. The garden designer must take full advantage of his ingenuity and creativity in the arrangement of time so that a visitor may find the right moment to make a turn, to look into the distance or to enjoy a wonderful view.

CHAPTER 5
COLORFUL SCENES

Buildings, hills, ponds, flowers and plants combine to present an elegant work of art—a scholar-designed picturesque garden with poetic charm and beautiful landscape.

Rockery Building

Rockeries are the skeleton structure of a garden. China's classical gardens often boast artificially piled rockeries in different scales, sizes and styles. As a matter of fact, rockeries are artificial. But, on the contrary, they are artistically true because every rockery is the artistic reproduction of a typical real hill or mountain through a process of artistic refinement and generalization.

Ancient Chinese rockery builders modeled on the real peak, slope, cliff and valley to design top-quality rockeries, which are acclaimed as top-notch artistic works.

Water Handling

Water plays a very important role in China's gardens, not only because it, complemented by hills, rockeries, trees and buildings, can present constantly changing scenery, but also because it can enrich the tour programs, such as picking lotus seeds, angling, boating and drinking by picking up floating wine-filled cups.

The most common body of water in a fairly large garden is a lake with a vast water surface. Small gardens are usually decorated with ponds,

A Full View of the Duixiu Hill of the Forbidden City in Beijing

The Duixiu (which means "beauty piling") Hill is situated in the imperial garden of the Forbidden City. Its name comes from the rockery builders who adopted the "beauty-piling" method when building this artificial hill, which was created by piling up rocks of distorted shapes. Standing in the imperial pavilion at the top of the mountain gives a bird's-eye view of the whole imperial garden, along with the distant views of the Forbidden City, the Jing Hill and the Xiyuan district.

The Huan Xiu Shan Zhuang (Mountain Villa Surounded by Flourishing Greenery) of Suzhou

The rockeries in the Huan Xiu Shan Zhuang cover an area of only half a *mu* (a *mu* equals to about 1/12 of an acre), yet they look like countless mountains and valleys. When you walk around the rockeries, you will find that the landscape changes constantly. The highest peak stands out in the southeast and is contrasted by the secondary peak in the northwest. They are surrounded by a pond and covered with green trees. The artificial hill is decorated with all the elements of a real mountain–hazardous paths, caves, secluded valleys, rock cliffs, ridges and precipices.

The Garden Rock in the Leshou Hall of the Summer Palace in Beijing

In addition to artificially piled hills in China's classical gardens, there are symbolic rockeries or the variant of a rockery that looks like a carved single-rock peak. Its special grain and lines, as well as its natural posture, are a beautiful visual feast to visitors.

The Rockeries of the Summer Palace in Beijing

The piling up of rocks to build rockeries is a creative art. The first step is to work out a draft in your mind by comparing all the distinctive natural mountains. Then you must have a good mastery of rock-piling techniques. Only in this way can you build magnificently conceived rockeries that are at once true to life and rich in artistic ambience.

The Yellow-stone Rockeries of the Yi He Yuan (Summer Palace) in Beijing

The Summer Palace is famous for two kinds of artificial hills–the Taihu-rock rockery and the yellow-stone rockery. For the latter, it is easy to build a foundation, but difficult to build the top. And for the former, it is vice versa. The yellow-stone rockery is characterized by bold and vigorous touches that display natural and graceful subtlety, whereas the Taihu-rock rockery is bold and virgorous with natural and graceful touches.

The Zhouyun Hill of Suzhou

The Zhouyong Hill of Suzhou is one of the most famous artificial hills built with Taihu rocks, which comes from the Taihu Lake and is a kind of limestone that has been corroded by the effects of water. This kind of porous rock, known for its "thin, wrinkly, leaky and seeping" characteristics, comes in an abundance of shapes.

The Rear Lake of the Yi He Yuan (Summer Palace) in Beijing

The bodies of water in gardens vary in size. Some are close to each other and others are scattered. But the most common layout is an orderly distribution of harmonious combinations of different sizes. Generally speaking, waterbodies are mainly arranged close together with only a few scattered. The concentrated arrangement makes the water surface look vast and extensive. Scattered ones surround the main waterbodies. The contrast between the two presents varied and attractive water scenery.

The Cup-floating Canal in the Xishang Pavilion of the Forbidden City in Beijing

This is a typical water scene of floating cups on a winding canal, which also serves as a kind of drinking game in ancient China. Scholars and poets express their sentiments by reciting poems and verses over cups of wine that they pick up from the winding man-dug stone canal.

creeks, moats, wellsprings and waterfalls. Some ponds are in natural shapes and some are in orderly shapes.

Distinctive Features of Buildings

Buildings are one of the most important elements in China's classical gardens. The poetic ambience and picturesque beauty of a garden are, for the most part, attributed to its buildings and their inspirational embellishments. The style of a garden, whether imperial, scholarly or folk, depends largely on the architectural style of the buildings in a garden.

A garden is decorated with a great variety of buildings. They can be categorized into the following main groups: halls, verandas, towers, boat-shaped halls, pavilions, corridors, bridges, walls and accessorial buildings.

Halls. Halls are also known as palaces in the imperial gardens of northern China. As the principal structure of a garden, the hall is used by the host to entertain his guests. If a hall is open on four sides and constitutes part of a spacious picturesque landscape, it is called a "four-facet hall." If the southern side of a hall is separated from the northern side by a screen-like partition, this kind of hall is called a "couple hall." The southern part is used in winter and spring while the northern part is used in autumn and summer. If a hall faces an enclosed courtyard without a pond that is decorated with only flowers and rocks, it is called literally a "flowery hall."

Verandas. Though not big in size, the elaborately decorated verandas are usually great in number. Attached to the rockery, pond, flowerbed or a grove of trees, they are harmoniously integrated into the environment.

The Pavilions, Terraces and Towers in the Summer Palace of Beijing

Groups of pavilions, terraces and towers lie between the rippling blue Kunming Lake and green wooded Longevity Hill in the Summer Palace. Their splendid, elegant and graceful look shows off the magnificent style of an imperial garden.

The Interior Decoration of Suzhou's Gardens

The traditional Chinese wood structure has been fine tuned for thousands of years. The garden builders refined their building techniques by mastering the novel concept of mono-unit shaping. As a result, the interior and exterior of their buildings are elegant, but the patterns are not elaborate.

The Momiao Veranda of the Xiequ Garden in the Summer Palace of Beijing

In Chinese "xuan" means a terraced veranda and "xie" means a ground veranda. "Xuan" stands at a distance at the top of a hill or on a high terrace overlooking the land or a pond. "Xie" usually rests relaxed on the waterside or against a backdrop of flowers.

The Interior Arrangement of Suzhou's Gardens

The traditional Chinese wood structure with unhidden wooden component parts demonstrates its bold and graceful lines. The rooms are tastefully and elegantly furnished and adorned to suit different tastes.

Xi Jia Lou of the Summer Palace in Beijing
In Chinese "lou" is a horizontal building without a platform or waist eaves and "ge" is a collective building with a platform. Standing in "lou" one can enjoy only a one-sided view. However, standing on the platform of "ge", one can enjoy distant views in all directions.

Towers. As the highest building in a garden, the tower is an ideal place for visitors to ascend enough height to enjoy a distant view. In the meantime the tower itself constitutes an important factor in garden designing for the purpose of adding the gradation of garden landscape.

Boat-shaped Hall. Boat-shaped hall is also known as "land boats," or "moor-free boats." This special type of building in a garden originated from the ancient gaily-painted pleasure boats or towered ships.

Pavilions. The Chinese character "ting" can also mean "stall." So a pavilion is built as a place where visitors can stop to rest, enjoy both the surrounding and distant views or ponder over the foregoing tour. In

The Marble Boat of the Summer Palace in Beijing

There are two different styles of boat-shaped hall. One is the exact copy of an elaborately carved pleasure boat built on the water. The Marble Boat of the Summer Palace is typical of this type.

The Xiangzhou Boat-shaped Hall of the Zhuo Zheng Yuan (Humble Administrator's Garden) in Suzhou

Another type of boat-shaped hall is built by the waterside, aspiring to capture the spirit of a boat. This kind of stone boat is composed of three sections: the front cabin is a high and open veranda; the middle cabin is a low and flat waterside veranda; the rear cabin is a two-storied tower. The Xiangzhou Boat-shaped Hall of the Humble Administrator's Garden is an example of this type.

The Fan-shaped Pavilion of the Shi Zi Lin (Lion Grove) in Suzhou

Chinese pavilions come in various shapes: long, square, round, triangular, pentagonal, hexagonal, octagonal, single-eaves, double-eaves, fan-shaped pavilions and even a half pavilion leaning against the wall.

addition, a pavilion itself is a tasteful adornment to the whole landscape of a garden.

Corridors. Corridors in a garden serve as a link between different buildings and scenes, thus playing the role of a tourist guide. The covered corridors can keep off the sun and rain. They also serve as a boundary or a partition between scenes.

Walls. Walls are divided into two categories—boundary walls and internal walls. The high boundary walls are used to enclose the whole garden and make it an independent entity endowed with the beauties of nature even in the center of a city. The internal walls, small and exquisite in different shapes, are used to separate space and scenes and create an environment of "a garden within a garden" and "a scene within a scene."

The Wulong (Five Dragons) Pavilions of the Beihai Park in Beijing

Small and exquisite pavilions are pleasant complements to hills, ponds, flowers or plants. Instead of stealing the show from other scenes, pavilions can add the touch that brings the whole garden landscape to life. That's why the location of a pavilion is unrestricted. It can be built among the flowers, by the roadside, at the top of a hill or on the shore of a pond.

The Long Corridor of the Summer Palace in Beijing

In terms of shapes, corridors can be divided into open, warm, half and double-lane corridors. An open corridor is exposed on both sides and lined with low-lying walls or rail-guarded benches separated by pillars for visitors to rest on.

The Latticed Windows of Gardens in Suzhou

To avoid dullness, garden designers adopted the method of building holed doors, holed windows and pane-free windows on walls. The holed doors and holed windows are usually framed with water-stone polished tiles. The contrasting grey-and-white color gives them a quiet elegance. They are built to connect the garden space on both sides of the wall. If you look through the holed window, you will be drawn to various three-dimensional paintings.

The Winding Corridor of the Liu Yuan (Lingering Garden) in Suzhou

In terms of its general shape and its integration with the topographic environment, corridors can be categorized into straight, zigzag, winding, climbing, waterside, serried and bridge-connected corridors.

The Walls of Gardens in Suzhou
The construction of walls has a special landscaping purpose. The walls of gardens are usually undulating and meandering according to the varied terrain so that they don't look stiff or rigid. The different shapes of walls, such as terraced walls and circular walls, often add vividness to the garden landscape.

Bridges. Bridges are used as an instrument to cross creeks and brooks, but they act as an important landscaping element as well. Bridges can be divided into arch bridges, flat bridges, pavilion bridges and covered bridges.

Flowers and Plants. The famous garden-building work *The Craft of Gardens* notes: "The shadow of phoenix trees should cover the ground, the shade of pagoda trees pattern the walls. Willows should be set along the embankments, plum trees around the buildings; reeds should be planted among the bamboos." This short passage vividly reveals the relationship between plants and the garden landscape. Plants are grown in different ways according to their different natural posture—group planting, planting in thick growth or isolated planting.

The Five-pavilion Bridge in the Shou Xi Hu (Slender West Lake) of Yangzhou

A pavilion bridge is a pavilion built on a bridge. The most famous pavilion bridge is the Five-pavilion Bridge in the Slender West Lake of Yangzhou. Both the covered bridge and the pavilion bridge serve a dual capacity as a path and a scene. Furthermore, they perform the function of a veranda where visitors can rest.

The Jade Belt Bridge of the Summer Palace in Beijing

The Jade Belt Bridge on the Western Shore of the Summer Palace in Beijing is a beautifully shaped stone arch bridge. Its egg-shaped upright arch and its double-curvature inverted-parabolic bridge floor have graceful lines and a very spectacular look. The upper part and railing of the bridge, made of carved white marble, are especially elegant and refined.

The Lotus and Carp Seen from the Xiaocanglang Pavilion in the Humble Administrator's Garden of Suzhou

Certain flowers and plants in China's classical gardens represent the ideal personality of an individual. For example, the pine, the bamboo and the plum are hailed as "three friends in winter" and symbolize pride and aloofness. The lotus is a symbol of a gentleman who "emerges unsullied from the filth." The implied meaning is that "a gentleman should keep his moral integrity intact in spite of general corruption."

The Covered Bridge of the Yu Yin Shan Fang (Mountain Cottage of Abundant Shade) in Guangdong Province

A covered bridge is a corridor built on a bridge or a section of corridor used as a bridge. The Huanhong-kualü Covered Bridge in the Yu Yin Shan Fang of Guangdong Province is typical of its kind.

CHAPTER 6

A FINE DISPLAY OF FAMOUS CLASSICAL GARDENS

As part of the important heritage to its civilization, China's gardens, with a long history and unique garden-building art, provide to the world a group of famous classic gardens.

1. Yuan Ming Yuan (Old Summer Palace)

The construction of the Old Summer Palace started in 1709. During the reign of Emperor Qianlong of the Qing dynasty, the Changchun Garden and the Wanchun Garden were built respectively to its east and to its south. Together they are called "the three gardens of Yuanming."

As the permanent residence of emperors, the Old Summer Palace serves a dual purpose as a palace and a garden. The buildings on the southern side of the Front Lake compose the zone of imperial palace. The gardens on the northern side of the Rear Lake form a large imperial garden. At the entrance of the Old Summer Palace lies the zone of imperial palace. The front section is the courtiers' waiting room. After you enter the main gate and cross the stone bridge, you'll see the plain and natural unadorned Zhengda-guangming Hall with a spacious square in front of it. Qinzheng Hall and Qinxian Hall stand on its left side and Baohe Hall and Taihe Hall stand on its right side. There is a forest of high rocks to its north with the Front Lake located further north. Jiuzhou-qingyan Hall, the centerpiece of the whole garden, faces the northern shore of the lake.

The imperial garden is composed of two distinctive scenic spots— the Fuhai Scenic Spot and the Rear Lake Scenic Spot. The Fuhai Scenic

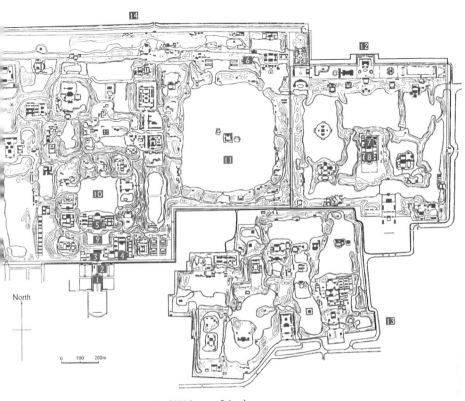

A General Plan of the Yuan Ming Yuan (Old Summer Palace)

The northwestern outskirts of Beijing used to be a natural countryside with a crisscross of spring-fed streams and flocks of hovering birds. Starting from the Liao (916 - 1125) and Jin (1115 - 1234) dynasties, emperors and senior officials built provincial imperial palaces and villa-attached gardens. The Qing dynasty witnessed a flourishing period of garden building. The most famous "three hills and five gardens" were built then–the Jingyi Garden on the Fragrant Hill, the Jingming Garden on the Jade Spring Hill, the Qingyi Garden (renamed "Yi He Yuan" or "Summer Palace" afterwards) on the Longevity Hill, the Yuan Ming Yuan (Old Summer Palace) and the Changchun Garden. Of the five gardens, the Old Summer Palace was known as the number one out of the ten thousand gardens for its biggest scope and imposing grandeur.

1. Main Gate of the Old Summer Palace 2. Churu-xianliang Gate 3. Zhengda-guangming Hall 4. Qinzheng-qingxian Hall 5. The Jiuzhou-qingyan Hall 6. Fanghu Beautiful Scenery 7. Chunhua Veranda 8. Yunzhen Study 9. Front Lake 10. Rear Lake 11. Fuhai Lake 12. Changchun Garden 13. Wanchun Garden 14. Yuan Ming Yuan

Spot is vast and open and has a square lake that is as long as 600 meters. The islands built in the lake are complemented by the reflection of a chain of peaks of the Western Hills outside the Old Summer Palace. The Rear Lake Scenic Spot is situated on the central axis of the Old Summer Palace. It is famous for its orderly but variable layout. The most important architectural complex—Jiuzhou-qingyan Hall—is part of this scenic spot.

The "exercising control of whole China" was conceptualized by the feudal emperors in the building of imperial gardens. As it is commonly acknowledged that China is composed of nine administrative divisions, the emperors have nine islands built in the lake to symbolize the nine divisions. Jiuzhou-qingyan Hall is built on the biggest island where the residence of the empress and empress dowager is located. Two emperors were born and died here.

The Changchun Garden consists of the principal southern scenic spot and the northern scenic spot. The waterbody of the southern scenic spot is divided into different size and style sections by islands, islets, bridges and causeways. The main buildings such as the Chunhua Veranda and Yunzhen Study are situated on the Zhongzhou Island. This island and Zelan Hall on the northern shore of the lake form the central axis of the garden. The southern and northern shorelines of the lake and the islets in the lake are dotted with sparsely grouped buildings. The northern scenic spot is known for its distinctive European-style buildings, hence the name "Europeans Buildings District."

The Wanchun Garden, formerly called the "Qichun Garden," is composed of many small gardens. Many small waterbodies combine to produce beautiful water scenery. The independent small gardens are the main tourist attractions.

Fanghu Beautiful Scenery in the Old Summer Palace

The Fanghu Beautiful Scenery is situated inside the northeastern shore of the Fuhai Lake. This scenic spot was built in 1740 and the most beautiful architectural complexes were concentrated here. The fork-shaped three multi-eaves pavilions in the front part of the scenic spot stuck out into the lake. Enshrined in the nine towers in the mid-rear part were over 2000 Buddha statues and more than 30 Buddhist pagodas. The magnificent and splendid tower building was actually a huge temple that symbolized a jewel palace on the immortals' hill.

Attractive water scenery is the focus of the three gardens of Yuan Ming Yuan. The gardens are scattered with lakes, ponds, canals and ditches. The waterbodies are dotted with islands and islets and rockeries and hillocks are spread about. All this has made the Yuan Ming Yuan look like a beautiful region of rivers and lakes in the south of the Yangtze River.

Countless buildings of different types and layouts, complemented by natural hills, lakes, trees and flowers, constitute a series of colorful and distinctive sights with a harmonious combination of architectural

"European Buildings District" of Yuan Ming Yuan

The northern scenic spot of the Changchun Garden is known as the "European Buildings District." It was designed by the Italian missionary Giuseppe Castiglione (1688 - 1766), who was appointed as an imperial painter working in the inner court. The whole district is lined up with six buildings, three sets of big fountains, several small fountains and some accessorial garden buildings. The main buildings are modeled on the baroque-style and rococo-style architecture fashionable in the late period of the Renaissance in Europe. But the details and adornment of the buildings have traditional Chinese characteristics. As a result, these buildings are considered as renowned examples of the successful introduction of West European architecture. Some historical remains still exist.

beauty and natural beauty. There are about 100 such beautiful sights in the Old Summer Palace and 30 of each in the Changchun Garden and in the Wanchun Garden. The names of all these sights are inscribed. The inscriptions of the 40 must-see sights in the Old Summer Palace and the 30 must-see sights in the Wanchun Garden are even accompanied by the poems written by emperors.

The buildings in the scenic spots are arranged in separate courtyards. Together with the surrounding hills, ponds, flowers and trees, they form distinctive scenes in varying sizes. These scenes are mostly presented in the form of "a garden within a garden" separated by rockeries or plants. The winding rivers and paths, which connect these scenes, guide the visitors from one sight to another. Some of these sights are copies of the beautiful scenes in the south of the Yangtze River and some are created according to the artistic ambience of ancient poems and paintings. Except a tiny number of halls and temples, the outward appearance of the buildings in the Old Summer Palace is unassuming and tasteful. Their exterior is seldom decorated with colored drawings and colored patterns. As a result their style is in perfect harmony with the natural environment of the garden. However, the interior decoration of these buildings is very elaborate and luxurious.

In September 1860 the Anglo-French Allied Forces invaded Beijing and burnt down the Old Summer Palace. The world-famous garden whose building and management had consumed a lot of financial, human and material resources during the past 150 years fell into ruin. Only a dozen of sights remained intact. When the Eight-power Allied Forces launched an invasion in 1900, the Old Summer Palace was ransacked again. There was nothing left but desolate and run-down ruins.

2. Yi He Yuan (Summer Palace)

The Summer Palace lies on the northwestern outskirts of Beijing. It was first built in 1750 and was burnt down by the Anglo-French Allied Forces in 1860. In 1884, to celebrate her birthday, the Empress Dowager Cixi had it rebuilt by diverting the funds earmarked for the navy and named it "Yi He Yuan" (also known as the Summer Palace).

The Summer Palace is composed of three areas, i.e., the area of Eastern Palace Gate and Imperial Mansions, the area of the Front Hill and Front Lake, and the area of the Rear Hill and Rear Lake.

As soon as visitors enter the Eastern Palace Gate, they will find themselves in a complex of palaces and halls. One of them is the Renshou Hall where the emperor gave an audience to his subordinate officials. Walking out of the Renshou Hall and stepping onto the Long Corridor will bring visitors into the area of the Front Hill and Front Lake. The green wooded Longevity Hill stands to the north of the Long Corridor. To its south lies the rippling blue of Kunming Lake. The winding Long Corridor extends between the foot of the Longevity Hill and the shoreline of the Kunming Lake from the Shizhang Pavilion in the west to the Yaoyue Gate in the east. The 728 meter long corridor is divided into 273 units. The horizontal link, which stretches across the Front Hill, and the vertical central axis combine to weave the network of the buildings on the Front Hill. Together with the white marble railing along the shoreline of the lake, the corridor serves as a borderline between the hill and the lake. At the same time it also gives an indication to the height of the hill. Against the backdrop of the Long Corridor and the white marble railing, the Longevity Hill, which is wooded with pine and cypress and lined with splendid halls, looks like a fabled mountain of the immortals. Visitors are

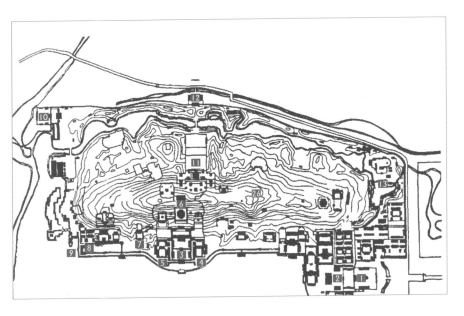

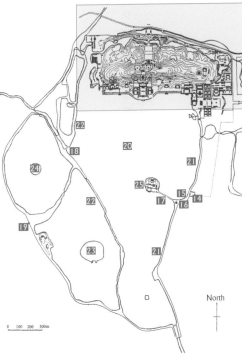

A General Plan of the Summer Palace

The Summer Palace is a garden of natural landscape with the Longevity Hill and the Kunming Lake as its principal structure and the Buddhist temple as its center. It covers an area of 1.31 square miles. Though it does not rank first in scope among the "three hills and five gardens", it has a distinctive style of its own in terms of natural landscape.

1. Eastern Palace Gate 2. Renshou Hall 3. Paiyun Hall 4. Jieshou Hall 5. Qinghua Veranda 6. Foxiang Tower 7. Yunsongchao Courtyard 8. Shizhang Pavilion 9. Marble Boat 10. Northwestern Gate 11. Xumilingjing Lamasery 12. Northern Palace Gate 13. Xiequ Garden 14. New Palace Gate 15. Bronze Bull 16. Kuoru Pavilion 17. Seventeen-arch Long Bridge 18. Jade Belt Bridge 19. Western Palace Gate 20. Kunming Lake 21. Eastern Shore 22. Western Shore 23. Zaojiantang Island 24. Zhijingge Island 25. Nanhu Island 26. Longevity Hill

Front Hill and Front Lake of the Summer Palace
Right at the top of the Longevity Hill stands the four-story high octagonal Foxiang Tower (Tower of the Fragrance of the Buddha). With the Paiyun Hall in front and the Sea-of-Wisdom Temple at the back, and the Baoyun Tower in the left and the Zhuanluncang Pagoda in the right, the Foxiang Tower and its splendid attached halls, towers and courtyards combine to form a sightseeing central axis running from the top of the Front Hill to its foot. This imposing architectural complex has become the centerpiece of the whole landscape of the Summer Palace.

treated to views of the majestic hill in the north and the graceful lake in the south when they roam along the Long Corridor. They can also stop to examine the beams of the Long Corridor, which are painted with more than 8000 color paintings of figures, landscapes, flowers and birds in the traditional Suzhou style. These paintings are so enchanting that the Long Corridor is also known as "a gallery of paintings."

A long causeway into the South Lake and the West Lake divides the Kunming Lake. Of the six bridges on the long causeway, the Jade Belt Bridge is the most famous. In contrast to the vast South Lake, the West Lake, which lies to the west of the long causeway, is quite small. The West Lake itself is divided into two parts. The southern part and the

Seventeen-arch Bridge of the Summer Palace

As the principal scenic spot of the Front Lake, the South Lake is open and wide with an islet built in its center. Serving as a link between the islet and the Kuoru Pavilion on the eastern shoreline, the elegantly shaped seventeen-arch bridge looks like a rainbow lying on the ripples or a dragon climbing the water. The partition of the South Lake by this eye-catching bridge brings a unique visual effect of depth and transparency.

northern part are centered respectively by the Zaojiantang Island and the Zhijingge Island. As a matter of fact, the Kunming Lake is divided into three waterbodies. Different in size and in degree of convergence, the three sections form independent scenes. But they are also closely linked and combine to make the Front Lake a tourist attraction with many must-see sights.

Walking westward along the Long Corridor will lead visitors to the Scenic Spot of the Rear Hill and Rear Lake. A long valley distinguishes this scenic spot with a lake sandwiched by two hills. The hill on the northern shore of the lake is an artificial one while the southern hill is a real one. The northern hill zigzags and meanders in accordance with the

Xiequ Garden of the Summer Palace

The Xiequ Garden (Garden of Harmonious Interest) has a style of its own in the Summer Palace. Its compact layout and refined decoration make it one of the most attractive gardens. Visitors are especially fond of this elegant and delicate garden because not only is it a bona fide imperial garden, it is also typical of the private gardens in the south of the Yangtze River.

alignment of the southern hill. It looks as if the Rear Lake has carved the hill into two, thus creating a deep and serene atmosphere of a valley. This section of the lake is long, narrow and zigzags. It widens and narrows to form an open and fluid waterbody. The shape of the waterbody changes in an orderly way to display the full rhythm and prosody of a long and narrow space. Because of the alignment of the two hills, the Rear Lake seems to be longer than it is. The narrow and serene Rear Lake sandwiched by two densely wooded hills adds a sharp contrast to the open and spacious Front Lake.

The principal buildings on the Rear Hill include the Back Temple Complex (a magnificent, splendid and solemn religious construction in the mixed Han and Tibetan style), an interesting and traditional Market Street and seven groups of garden architecture scattered on both shorelines. In the middle of the Market Street is a big stone bridge across

Kunming Lake in the Summer Palace

Islets allow visitors' fancies to roam, as they are usually associated with the mountains of the immortals. Islets are usually built in a big lake to add to the gradation of the landscape and incorporating them into a pond is a common approach for garden designers to create beautiful water scenery in classical gardens.

the lake. The bridge faces the Northern Palace Gate in the north and looks southward beyond the Song Hall on to the Xumi-lingjing Lamasery on the two-storied foundation and the Xiangyan-zongyin Buddhist Temple behind it, thus forming a central axis of the Rear Hill. Meeting the Rear Lake at right angles, the central axis of the Rear Hill corresponds with that of the Front Hill. The Xiangyan-zongyin Buddhist Temple is surrounded by Tibetan-style red terraces on which 12 blockhouse-like structures are arranged in strict order, giving it an imposingly religious grandeur.

The Xiequ Garden to the east of the Rear Lake is also called the Huishan Garden because it was modeled on the Ji Chang Yuan (Garden of Lodging One's Expansive Feelings) at the foot of the Huishan Hill in Wuxi. This garden is composed of the Water Garden in the south and the Jiqing Veranda in the north.

3. Bi Shu Shan Zhuang
   (Chengde Mountain Resort)

Emperor Kangxi of Qing dynasty and his successors made an inspection tour of the north every year. In order to meet the political requirements and satisfy the needs of leisure living outside the capital city, the emperor gave orders in 1701 to build a complex of palaces to escape the summer heat in Beijing, hence the Chengde Mountain Resort (also known as Rehe Temporary Imperial Palace or Chengde Provisional Imperial Palace). Its construction began in Shangying, Rehe (i.e., present-day Chengde of Hebei Province), which was surrounded by undulating mountain ranges, lingering waters, cool environment and picturesque scenery. It took more than 80 years to complete the whole project and its final extension was built in 1790. It is China's largest existing imperial garden. As the resort was warm in winter and cool in summer, the emperors from Kangxi (the second emperor of the Qing dynasty) to Xianfeng (the seventh emperor of the Qing dynasty) spent almost half a year anually at this resort. While escaping the summer heat in the capital city of Beijing, the emperors handled administrative affairs and received noblemen, ministers and foreign envoys here. In fact, Chengde became the second administrative center of the Qing government. The Mountain Resort is surrounded by a 6 mile long outer wall. The beauty of its landscape is beyond description. The most famous scenic spots are the 36 sights that Emperor Kangxi and Emperor Qianlong each named.

Lizheng Gate is the main entrance in the western wall. The nine-courtyard compound behind the gate is the principal palace where the emperor lived and handled administrative affairs. The nine-room wide Danbo-zhicheng Hall is the principal hall in the principal palace and

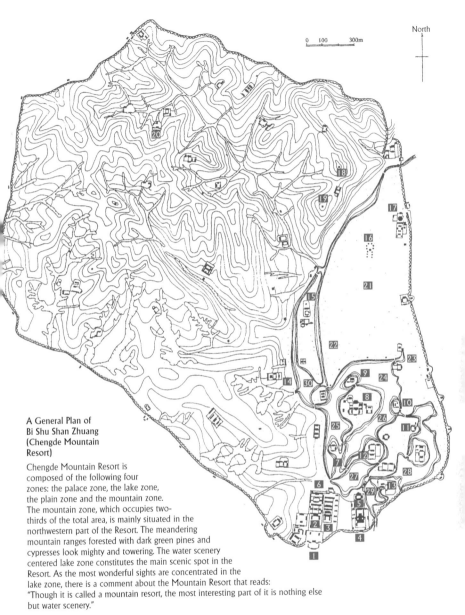

0 100   300m

North

A General Plan of
Bi Shu Shan Zhuang
(Chengde Mountain
Resort)

Chengde Mountain Resort is
composed of the following four
zones: the palace zone, the lake zone,
the plain zone and the mountain zone.
The mountain zone, which occupies two-
thirds of the total area, is mainly situated in the
northwestern part of the Resort. The meandering
mountain ranges forested with dark green pines and
cypresses look mighty and towering. The water scenery
centered lake zone constitutes the main scenic spot in the
Resort. As the most wonderful sights are concentrated in the
lake zone, there is a comment about the Mountain Resort that reads:
"Though it is called a mountain resort, the most interesting part of it is nothing else
but water scenery."

1. Lizheng Gate 2. Principal Palace 3. Songhe Chambers 4. Dehui Gate 5. Eastern Palace 6. Wanhe-Songfeng
Hall 7. Zhijingyun Causeway 8. Ruyizhou Island 9. Yanyu Tower 10. Jinshan Pavilion 11. Huashen Temple
12. Yuese-jiangsheng Island 13. Wenyuan Lion Forest Garden 14. Shuyuan Temple 15. Wenjin Tower 16. Yurt
17. Yongyou Temple 18. Double Peaks in the North 19. Nanshan-jixue Pavilion 20. Bijing Hall 21. Wanshu
Garden 22. Shimadai Scenic Spot 23. Rehe Spring 24. Cheng Lake 25. Ruyi Lake 26. Upper Lake 27. Lower
Lake 28. Jing Lake (or Mirror Lake) 29. Yin Lake (or Silver Lake) 30. Chang Lake (or Long Lake)

was used to celebrate important festivals and hold grand ceremonies. All the wooden parts of the hall were made of *nanmu* (a kind of fragrant fine-grained hardwood) so that the hall was also called "Nanmu Hall." The Yiqingkuang Hall stands behind the Nunmu Hall and served as a place where the emperor gave an audience to his ministers. The actions of daily life in the solemn and quiet principal palace imbued it with a sense of amiable intimacy. Every courtyard is decorated with rockery, pine and cypress. The serene and pleasant environment is typical of an imperial palace built outside the capital. Situated to the east of the principal palace is the Songhe Chambers where the empress and imperial concubines lived. Located to the east of the Songhe Chambers was the Eastern Palace where the crown prince lived. Unfortunately, it was completely destroyed in a later period. When visitors step out of the Xiuyun Gate, they will find themselves in a landscaped area.

The three tourist routes of the lake zone, while serving as a link to the attractive sights, carves up the lake into several distinctive scenic spots of different sizes. The middle route starts at the Wanhe-Songfeng Hall and reaches the Zhijingyun Causeway. On the way one can visit the Yuese-jiangsheng Island, the Ruyizhou Island and the Yanyu Tower. With red pillars, grey tiles and a surrounding corridor, the Yanyu Tower was modeled on the Tower of Mist and Rain in Jiaxing of Zhejiang Province. The Qingyang Study on its left side and the Duishan Study on its right side flank the courtyard in front of the tower. It is said that the latter was Emperor Qianlong's study and his favorite concubine Li once used the former study to paint and recite poems. The Shuixin Pavilions (actually a triple-pavilion bridge) is the starting point of the east tourist route. Walking northward from the Juan'a Beautiful Scenery, one can climb a stone bridge across the lake and catch sight of the triple

The Yuese-jiangsheng Island of Chengde Mountain Resort

There are three main tourist routes in the lake zone. The middle route starts from Wanhe-Songfeng Hall and reaches the Zhijingyun Causeway. The Zhijingyun Causeway is modeled on the Su Causeway in the West Lake of Hangzhou. The tip of the causeway is divided into three prongs leading to the three islands in the lake. On the Yuese-jiangsheng Island the Jingji Study, the Yingxin Study, the long corridor and pavilions are all hidden in the green trees, which looks like a beautiful scene from the south of the Yangtze River.

pavilions. Their reflection on the rippled water is unspeakably beautiful and the fragrance of lotus is pleasantly refreshing. Further northward is the quiet and secluded East Lake. Situated to its north are the Jinshan Pavilion and the Rehe Spring.

The mountain zone is located in the west of the Resort. The south-north meandering mountain ranges form a natural barrier. All the original buildings built on the mountain zone were destroyed. Only three newly built pavilions are scattered there. The Nanshan-jixue Pavilion stands at the top of the highest northern peak looking down on the Songyun Valley in front and leaning against the other two peaks.

The Songyun Valley of the Chengde Mountain Resort

Group planting is used in garden landscaping to give the impression of a covered forest. This landscaping technique was adopted in the building of imperial gardens and other huge gardens. The species of trees planted are either identical or varied. An identical set of trees is meant to overwhelm visitors by the broad scale of the forest, whereas a varied set intends to captivate.

The plain zone lies to the north of the lake zone. It used to be the place where the emperors of the Qing dynasty hosted picnics, received the Mongolian princes and noblemen, and enjoyed fireworks, horse racing and wrestling. In the western part of the plain zone is a Shimadai Scenic Spot with a carpet of lush green grass. The yurts and David's deer combine to present wonderful grassland scenery. The forest zone in the east is called the Wanshu Garden. It was originally planted with ancient elm trees, verdant pines, giant Chinese scholartrees and aged willows. This vast woodland, dotted with the Jiashu Veranda, the Chunhao Veranda, the Yongyou Temple and the Lecheng Tower, has a very pastoral appeal to it.

In addition to the majority of natural scenes in the Chengde Mountain Resort, some sights are unique in their own styles, constituting "a garden within a garden," such as the well known Bijing Hall and Wenyuan Lion Grove Garden. The garden art of the resort is distinguished by the fact that full attention is given to the change of its natural terrain. The scenic spots of different styles are refined and reorganized into an integrated whole. Taking the local circumstances into consideration, the Resort designers and builders created a mutually complementary landscape with an equal combination of joint and separate scenes along with primary and secondary scenes. Water scenery and mountain scenery are complementary to each other. The coherently designed buildings make the beautiful landscape even more beautiful. As a result, the landscaping of the mountain resort has reached the acme of perfection.

4. Bei Hai Gong Yuan (Beihai Park)

The Beihai (means "north sea") Park located to the west of the Palace Museum and the Jing Hill (also known as the Coal Hill) in Beijing, is one of the most famous existing imperial gardens. As early as the Jin dynasty (1115 – 1234) a provisional imperial palace called the Daning Palace was built on the Qionghua Island. During the Yuan dynasty (1279 – 1368) the Qionghua Island was renamed the Wansui (means "His majesty") Hill and the Taiye Pond. The capital city of the Yuan dynasty was built with the Qionghua Island as its center.

On the western side of Beihai there are two famous buildings: the Yuexin Hall where the emperor received his ministers and attended to administrative affairs and the Qingxiao Tower where the emperor enjoyed the spectacular winter sights of ice and snow. Located on the western shore of the island are the Linguang Hall and the Yuegu Hall. The inner walls of the Yuegu Hall are decorated with stone carvings of model calligraphy from the Sanxi Studio. The slope of the hill is dotted with rockeries and pavilions of various descriptions. On the northern side of the hill stretches a half-round Yanlou corridor consisting of 60 units, including the Yiqing Tower at the east end and the Fenmin Tower at the west end. Situated in between them are the two-storied Yilan Hall and Daoning Studio where one can enjoy the view of the White Dagoba in the south and look down on the rippled lake in the north. The northern slope is known for its scattered overhanging rocks, caves, pavilions and small houses. Some houses even have direct access to the caves. On the eastern side of the hill the East Gate, the Stone Bridge, the Memorial Arch and the Zhizhu Temple, dedicated to the Bodhisattva Manjusri, all combine to form a horizontal axis which crosses the principal axis. The

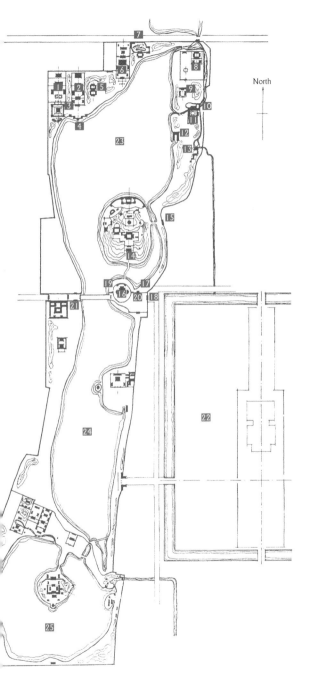

North

A General Plan of the Three Sea-named Lakes

After the Ming dynasty the Beihai (North Sea) Lake, the Zhonghai (Middle Sea) Lake and the Nanhai (South Sea) Lake were called the "three seas." During the reign of Emperor Shunzhi of the Qing dynasty the White Dagoba and Buddhist temples were built on Qionghua Island. During the reign of Emperor Qianlong of the Qing dynasty many landscaped buildings were erected on the northeastern shoreline of the lake. The White Dagoba on Qionghua Island serves as the center of the designing composition of Beihai Park. Beautiful sights are arranged on the island and along the shorelines of the lake, thus forming a water scenery centered landscape distinguished by a perfect blend of hill scenery and water scenery.

1. Wanfo Tower 2. Chanfu Temple 3. Sukhavati 4. Five Dragon Pavilions 5. Chengguan Hall 6. Xitian Dreamland 7. Jingqing Study 8. Xiancan Hall 9. Temple of the Dragon King 10. Guke Pavilion 11. Huafang Study 12. Lakeside Dock 13. Haopu Creek 14. Qionghua Island 15. Zhishan Gate 16. Circular City 17. Sangyuan Gate 18. Qianming Gate 19. Left Chengguang Gate 20. Right Chengguang Gate 21. Fuhua Gate 22. Forbidden City 23. Beihai (North Sea) 24. Zhonghai (Middle Sea) 25. Nanhai (South Sea)

Beihai Lake

On the southern slope of Wansui Hill in Beihai Park there is a principal axis starting from the White Dagoba, passing Liuli-shanyin Hall, Pu'an Hall, Zhengjue Hall, the Duiyun-jicui Memorial Arch, the Yong'an Stone Bridge, and reaching the Circular City.

Qiongdao-chunyin Stone Pillars are acclaimed as one of the eight must-sees in Beijing. The heads and foundations of the pillars and their railings are all elaborately carved.

The eastern and northern shores of the Beihai Lake are scattered with several courtyard compounds. The special garden constructions that are partly hidden and partly visible against the backdrop of the vast and sparkling Taiye Pond add to the tourist attractions of the northeastern shore of the Beihai Lake, which is enhanced by undulating hills. This scenic spot complements the distant towering White Dagoba and the imposing halls on Qionghua Island.

Linked with the southern shore of Qiongdao Island by the Yong'an Bridge is the Circular City—a round terraced city wall-like construction—where visitors can enjoy the beautiful view of the White Dagoba on the other side of the bridge.

5. Zhuo Zheng Yuan (Humble Administrator's Garden)

The Humble Administrator's Garden lies in the Dongbei Street inside the Lou Gate of Suzhou and covers an area of about 40,000 square meters, is one of the four most famous gardens in Suzhou. The garden was first built during the reign of Emperor Zhengde of the Ming dynasty. According to historical records, the Supervising Censor Wang Xianchen was dissatisfied with his official career and resigned to live a secluded life. Only then did he get the idea to build this garden. After reading the works of Pan Yue, a hermit of the Western Jin dynasty (265 – 316), Wang borrowed the wording from his prose entitled *Dwelling in Seclusion* and named the garden "the Humble Administrator's Garden" for the purpose of recounting a feudal scholar-official's determination to withdraw from society and live in solitude.

The principal building of the garden is Yuanxiang Hall, which was built in the traditional Chinese architectural style of the 4-slope-and-9-ridge saddle roof. Walking eastward from Yuanxiang Hall one can see a pavilion at the top of a hillock. At the foot of the hillock are elegant themed courtyards, such as Linglong Hall, the Jiashi Pavilion, the Tingyu Chamber, the Haitang-chunwu Terrace and Wuzhu-youju Residence. Walking westward from Yuanxiang Hall and turning south at the Yiyu Pavilion is a quiet and zigzag water-scenery courtyard. Across the long and twisting creek is a covered bridge and a bridge room. This special construction gives the impression that the modest creek is long and has a distant source. After crossing the bridge, the Lvyi Pavilion, Yulan Hall and the Xiangzhou Building will come into view. The Xiangzhou Building is a spectacular boat-shaped building which

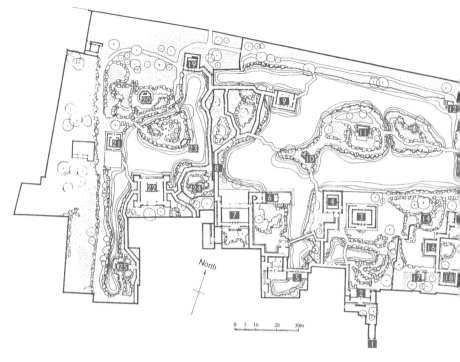

A Plan of the Central and Western Parts of the Zhuo Zheng Yuan (Humble Administrator's Garden)

The Humble Administrator's Garden is divided into three parts, i.e., the central, eastern and western parts. The principal sights are concentrated in the central part. When you enter the garden through the waist gate, you'll find yourself blocked by a barrier of rockeries. Only when you make a turn at the hillock will you find yourself facing a charming scene.

1. Garden Entrance 2. Waist Gate 3. Yuanxiang Hall 4. Yiyu Veranda 5. Xiaocanglang Pavilion 6. Xiangzhou Building 7. Yulan Hall 8. Bieyou-dongtian Pavilion 9. Jianshan Building 10. Hefeng Four-facet Pavilion 11. Xuexiang-yunwei Pavilion 12. Lvyi Pavilion 13. Wuzhu-youju Residence 14. Xiuqi Pavilion 15. Haitang-chunwu Terrace 16. Linglong Hall 17. Jiashi Pavilion 18. Tingyu Chamber 19. Daoying Building 20. Fucui Pavilion 21. Liuting Pavilion 22. House of 36 Mandarin Ducks 23. Yushui-tongzuo Veranda 24. Yiliang Pavilion 25. Taying Pavilion

stands opposite of the Hefeng-simian Pavilion in the middle of the pond and looks far into the Jianshan Building. The Xiangzhou Building is composed of the two-storied Chengguan Building in the west, a three-sided open tea pavilion in the east and the low central hall in the middle. The three parts are united as an integral whole with a harmonious combination of different heights and of reality and imagination. Seen

Zhuo Zheng Yuan (Humble Administrator's Garden)
The principal building of the Humble Administrator's Garden is Yuanxiang Hall with the Yiyu Veranda to its west and the lotus pond to its north. The three islets in the pond represent the three imaginary mountains of the immortals. There is a pavilion on each islet. The Xuexiang-yunwei Pavilion on the middle islet faces Yuanxiang Hall across the pond.

from the north, the Chengguan Building is high and solid with painted walls and carved windows and looks like a wheelhouse. Decorated on both sides with lattice windows, the central hall looks like a cabin. Open and unobstructed, the terrace in front of the pavilion looks like a deck on the bow. As the whole the building looks very much like a flamboyantly painted towered ship berthed alongside the shore.

At the western end of the garden is a half pavilion called "Bie You Dong Tian" (which means "a different world") along the long corridor against the wall to the north of Yulan Hall. After turning here and walking through a moon gate, you'll come to the Western Garden of the Humble Administrator's Garden. One can find many enjoyments here, such as appreciating the reflection of a pagoda in the rippled water from

The Yuanxiang Hall of the Humble Administrator's Garden in Suzhou

Halls are always the centerpieces of garden layouts and are usually situated in the best locations of the gardens. They have considerable heights and are ornately decorated. Because it is closely connected with the living quarters, a hall must have a favorable exposure that makes it easy to enjoy attractive views.

the Daoying Building, listening to the rain beating against the lotus leaves from the Liuting Pavilion, watching the floating green duckweed from the Fucui Pavilion, listening to cicadas and birds singing from the Taying Pavilion, take in the refreshing breeze from the Yushui-tongzuo Veranda, look at the hills and lakes outside the wall by climbing up to the Yiliang Pavilion, observe the mandarin ducks and ornamental fish playing in the water in the House of 36 Mandarin Ducks and smell the beautiful camellias and white-skinned pines in the House of 18 Datura Blossoms.

The Eastern Garden is situated at the eastern end of the Humble Administrator's Garden. It has few buildings, but its prominent features are its lush forest, natural environment, and open and distant scenery.

A Bird's-eye View of the Liu Yuan (Lingering Garden)

Of the gardens in Suzhou, the Lingering Garden is known for its ingenious arrangement of architectural space. You can enter the garden through He House and reach the central Hill and Pond Zone by passing Wufengxian Hall (No.1 District), Qingfeng Pond House and the Quxi Building. You can also enter the garden through the main entrance and reach the Eastern Garden by passing a winding corridor, the Quxi Building and Wufengxian Hall. Whichever route you take, you will feel a striking contrast in terms of size, brightness, spaciousness and height.

6. Liu Yuan (Lingering Garden)

The Lingering Garden is located outside the Chang Gate of Suzhou and was first built during the reign of Emperor Jiajing of the Ming dynasty. It is one of the four most famous gardens in Suzhou. The beams and pillars of Wufengxian Hall—the biggest building in the garden—are made from the *nanmu* wood, why is why it is also called Nanmu Hall. With a high and extended space and elegant decoration, the hall is considered as a masterpiece among the garden halls. Since the courtyards in front and at the back are both decorated with rockeries, people sitting in the hall feel like they are facing a rocky ravine. The rockeries in the front courtyard resemble the twelve animals each symbolizing the year of one's birth. Among the rockeries in the back courtyard is a pond where goldfish is raised for visitors' delight.

Some smaller secluded buildings and courtyards surround Wufengxian Hall: the Jigu-degeng Spot to its west, He House to its south and the Yifeng Pavilion and the Huanwo-dushu Study to its east. These tiny buildings add a nice contrast to the tall and sumptuous

The Guanyun Peak of the Liu Yuan (Lingering Garden)

Guanyun Peak is the highest rockery built with Taihu rocks in Suzhou. Its upright posture looks lofty and imposing. It is flanked by Ruiyun Peak in the east and Xiuyun Peak in the west.

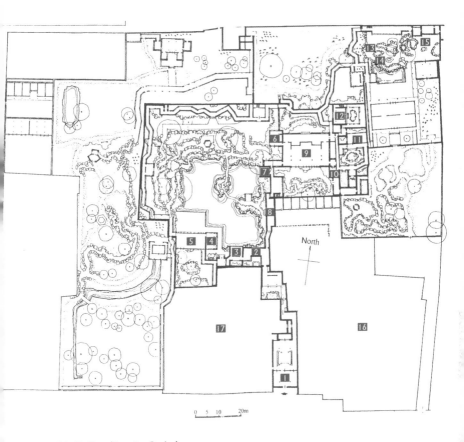

A Plan of the Liu Yuan (Lingering Garden)

The Lingering Garden, which covers an area of about two hectares, is divided into three parts, i.e., the central, eastern and western zones. The Central Zone, formerly called the Hanbi Mountain Villa, constitutes the principal scenic spot of the Lingering Garden. It can be further divided into the eastern section and the western section. The latter is characteristic of its beautiful hills and ponds whereas its spectacular buildings and courtyards distinguish the former.

1. Main Entrance 2. Gumu-jiaoke Ancient-tree Section 3. Green Shade 4. Mingse Building 5. Hanbi Mountain Villa 6. Jigu-degeng Spot 7. Qingfeng Pond House 8. Quxi Building 9. Wufengxian Hall 10. He House 11. Yifeng Pavilion 12. Huanwo-dushu Study 13. Xiuyun Peak 14. Guanyun Peak 15. Ruiyun Peak 16. Residential Quarters 17. Ancestral Hall

85

The Liu Yuan (Lingering Garden)

After you enter the garden through the side gate of the Hanbi Mountain Villa and walk past the winding corridor and the two enclosed courtyards, you'll find yourself at the southern boundary of the Hill and Pond Scenic Spot, i.e., the Gumu-jiaoke Ancient-tree Section. When you look through the pane-free windows, you can dimly see the beautiful landscape of hills, ponds and pavilions. Walking westward along the Ancient-tree Section, you can enjoy the beautiful scenes of the Lvyin Veranda, the Mingse Building and the Hanbi Mountain Villa on the shoreline. They also form an attractive architectural skyline on the southern shoreline of the pond.

Wufengxian Hall. Its rockeries and the surrounding corridor distinguish the courtyard where the Yifeng Pavilion stands. The area between the wall and the corridor is partitioned into small units decorated with Taihu rocks, stalagmites, bamboo and Basho, respectively, forming many small landscape paintings.

7. Wang Shi Yuan (Master of the Nets Garden)

The Wang Shi Yuan (Master of the Nets Garden), which is located in the Kuojiatou Street in the south of Suzhou, was first built during the reign of Emperor Qianlong of the Qing dynasty and later rebuilt during the reigns of Emprors Jiaqing and Daoguang. It covers an area of only 5 *mu*.

Visitors enter the garden through the Wangshi-xiaozhu Gate. They will reach the Xiaoshan-conggui Chamber after walking through a narrow winding corridor. Open on the four sides, the chamber faces Yun Hillock in the north. As this yellow-stone hillock lies on the shore and blocks the landscape, the big-sized Xuan Hall seems to recede out of the principal lake landscape, thus ensuring the open and wide effect of the lake. Just as the name "Xiaoshan-conggui" literally means "Osmanthus trees on a small hill," this scenic spot is mainly planted with osmanthus trees. After leaving the chamber and passing a low and narrow winding corridor, you'll reach the pond in the central part. As the name of the garden "wang shi" means "fisherman," the landscaping of this garden strive to depict the theme of "a secluded fisherman." As a result, the rippled lake, though it measures only about half a *mu*, gives the visitors an impression of a vast waterbody. There is an arm each at the southeastern and northwestern tips of the pond. The shoreline is decorated with rockeries, projecting rocks, fishing terrace, arch bridge and flagstone pulling bridge. All this presents a typical rippled lake with running water coming from an endless source. No lotus or other plants are grown in the pond, so that the varied reflections of the sky, hills, pavilions and trees enrich the landscape of the garden.

In the northwestern corner of the garden stands a courtyard called

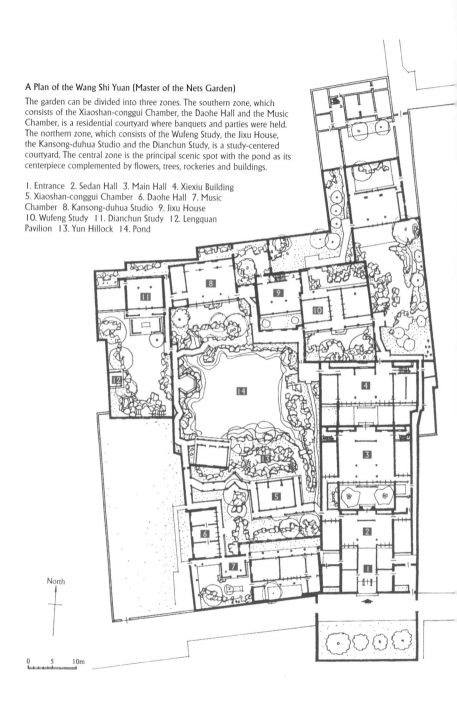

A Plan of the Wang Shi Yuan (Master of the Nets Garden)

The garden can be divided into three zones. The southern zone, which consists of the Xiaoshan-conggui Chamber, the Daohe Hall and the Music Chamber, is a residential courtyard where banquets and parties were held. The northern zone, which consists of the Wufeng Study, the Jixu House, the Kansong-duhua Studio and the Dianchun Study, is a study-centered courtyard. The central zone is the principal scenic spot with the pond as its centerpiece complemented by flowers, trees, rockeries and buildings.

1. Entrance 2. Sedan Hall 3. Main Hall 4. Xiexiu Building 5. Xiaoshan-conggui Chamber 6. Daohe Hall 7. Music Chamber 8. Kansong-duhua Studio 9. Jixu House 10. Wufeng Study 11. Dianchun Study 12. Lengquan Pavilion 13. Yun Hillock 14. Pond

North

0   5   10m

The Wang Shi Yuan (Master of the Nets Garden)

On the western shoreline lies a winding corridor with a pavilion called "Yuedao-fenglai (which means 'the moon and wind are approaching')" in it. Sitting in the pavilion, visitors can await the bright moon and gentle breeze while overlooking the change of water scenery. Opposite to the pavilion across the pond is a whitewashed wall on the eastern shoreline with an open corridor in front. Together with rockeries and vines, the northern shore looks like a Chinese ink-and-wash painting.

"Dianchun." This small courtyard looks like a landscape painting complete with towering rockeries, evenly spaced trees and a chilly spring. The Lengquan Pavilion is located beside the spring. Legend has it that the Lingbi Stone Tablet in the pavilion is a relic left behind by the famous painter Tang Bohu of the Ming dynasty. The Ming Garden built in the Metropolitan Museum of Art in New York is modeled on the Wang Shi Yuan. As a result, the Wang Shi Yuan is famous all over the world.

8. Shi Zi Lin (Lion Grove)

The Shi Zi Lin is located in the Yuanlin Road of Suzhou and was first built during the Yuan dynasty. With an area of about 12 *mu*, the Shi Zi Lin is distinguished by its beautiful water scenery. The pond lies in the central part and the principal buildings stand in the eastern and northern parts. A winding corridor surrounds the whole garden. The Yanyu Hall—the main hall of the garden—is built in the style of well-matched paired chambers. Behind the Yanyu Hall is the Xiaofang Hall. When you turn to the west, you'll climb a rockery to reach the principal building of the garden—the two-story Yifeng-zhibai Tower. The tower is linked to the front rockery by a stone bridge across the creek. You will find yourself on the rockery as you cross the bridge. Piled up with the Taihu rocks, the rockery looks like a mountain with towering ragged peaks, zigzag stone paths and countless connected caves. When you go into the maze-like caves, you'll find it difficult to get out unless you take the path in the right direction.

The Wusong (which literally means "five pine trees") Garden lies to the west of the Yifeng-zhibai Tower. The garden, decorated with five ancient pine trees and rockeries, is pleasantly quiet and secluded. In front of the garden is a lotus pond. The beautiful shoreline scenery is composed of the properly spaced buildings varying in heights: the Jianshan Building, the Hehua Hall, the Zhenqu Pavilion, the Anxiang-shuying Building and the Stone Boat, to name but a few. You can reach the Anxiang-shuying Building and the Rockeries in the western part of the garden by following the long corridor to the north of the stone boat. Walking southward from the Wenmei Pavilion and turning to the east at the Shuangxiangxian House, you'll be faced with the Fan-shaped

A Bird's-eye View of the Shi Zi Lin (Lion Grove)

The Lion Grove became famous thoughout China after the famous painter Ni Zan (1301 – 1374) of the Yuan dynasty created a scroll painting of it. Both Emperors Kangxi and Qianlong of the Qing dynasty visited this garden on their respective inspection tours of the south. Emperor Qianlong even gave orders to model the Wen Garden and the Changchun Garden in his provisional imperial palace in Rehe after the Lion Grove.

The Lion Grove

At the top of the artificial hill in the western part of the garden stands the Feipu Pavilion made of three layers of Taihu rocks. Next to it is the Wenmei Pavilion where you can get a panoramic view of the whole beautifully landscaped garden.

Pavilion and the elegantly arranged rockeries and bamboos behind it in the southwestern corner. Beyond the pavilion there is a long corridor along the south wall that reduces the sense of seclusion. The corridor rises and falls with the terrain and the winding stone paths are dotted with roadside half pavilions and rockeries of various shapes. Displayed on the walls of the corridor are stone carvings of the model calligraphy of famous calligraphers in ancient China. Toward its end the corridor branches into double lanes leading to the Lixue Hall. The partition wall between the double lanes of the corridor is decorated with pane-free windows of different shapes. Visitors can enjoy the colorful sights of the garden through these windows.

9. Cang Lang Ting (Blue Waves Pavilion)

The Blue Wave Pavilion is the oldest existing garden in Suzhou. It was originally the garden of a nobleman in the period of Five dynasties (907 – 960). Su Shunqin, a well-known scholar of the Northern Song dynasty purchased the garden and named it "Cang Lang Ting." The garden was deserted during the Yuan and Ming dynasties. It was renovated during the reign of Emperor Kangxi of the Qing dynasty and began to take the shape of its present-day garden. The Cang Lang Ting, which covers an area of about 16 *mu*, is one of the four most famous existing gardens in Suzhou.

Before entering the Northern Gate, you are faced with a zigzag bridge. A memorial arch at the end of the bridge is inscribed with four characters: "Cang Lang Sheng Ji" (which means "renowned historical site of Canglang"). As natural water scenery is available outside of the garden, the landscaping of the garden itself is focused on an artificial hill and its surrounding buildings. The western part of the artificial hill is piled up with delicately-shaped rockeries half encircling a pond. As the bank of the pond is high and the surface of the water is low, visitors will feel as though they are standing on the edge of a bottomless pit.

There is a winding corridor in the garden. After you enter the garden and walk southward along the west corridor, you will reach the southwestern courtyard. The beech with plentiful foliage in the courtyard is so big that you can only embrace it with your outstretched arms. Stories about historical figures are carved on the many bricks on the wall. Situated to its east are the Qingxiang Hall and the 500 Talented Celebrities Ancestral Hall. Located to its south are the Cuilinglong Chamber and the Kanshan Building. There are two

The Cang Lang Ting (Blue Waves Pavilion)

The eastern part of the hill is based on the original earth terrain and yellow stones to protect the slope strengthen the foot of the hill. The trail on the hill is paved. Covered with broad-leafed indocalamus and tall ancient trees, the hill looks like a remote forested mountain with the Cang Lang Ting hidden in the shade. The stone pillars of the square-shaped ancient pavilion are carved with a couplet to the effect of "The gentle breeze and bright moon are priceless; the nearby creek and distant mountain are sentient."

高猿滄

A Bird's-eye View of the Cang Lang Ting (Blue Wave Pavilion)

Of all the gardens in Suzhou, the Cang Lang Ting is distinguished by its simple and straightforward style. Different from other gardens, its water scenery lies outside of the garden. The shorelines are built with Taihu rocks and are planted with poplars, willows and peach trees. The outside and inside are partitioned with a corridor wall instead of a high wall. As a result, the outside scenery and the inside scenery merge into a complete landscape to creat an enhanced effect.

stone chambers on the ground floor of the Kanshan Building. The stone chambers are the most ideal place for visitors to sit on to cool themselves of the summer heat. The courtyard in front of the stone chambers is decorated with rockeries. The wall of the corridor is set with pane-free windows of different shapes through which visitors can enjoy the beautiful scenery inside or outside the garden from either side of the wall. Though partitioned by a wall, the landscape inside and outside the garden seems to be an integral whole. The latticed wall with pane-free windows of varied shapes and patterns has become a unique attraction to visitors.

10. Ji Chang Yuan (Garden for Lodging One's Expansive Feelings)

Located at the eastern foot of the Hui Hill and at the western foot of the Xi Hill in Wuxi, Jiangsu Province, the Ji Chang Yuan borders the Huishan Temple in the south. It was first built during the reign of Emperor Zhengde of the Ming dynasty and rebuilt in the late period of the Qing dynasty. The Ji Chang Yuan is considered as one of the famous gardens in the south of the Yangtze River.

As soon as you enter the garden, you are in front of the flowery hall. Behind it is a screen of rockeries. Once you walk through the cave of the artificial hill, a beautiful landscape unfolds before your eyes. The principal scene is a rippled pond called Jinhuiyi (which means "the rippled pond is as beautiful as brocade"). In the old days the pond was full of pleasure boats and wine shop boats. Their reflections on the rippled pond were as beautiful as brocade, hence the name. The open and broad pond forms a clear and extended space. Its western shoreline is decorated with a pair of imitated arms, a bridge and a beach, all of which are elegantly built with Taihu rocks.

The artificial hill on the western shoreline, which is arranged like a meandering mountain range with towering peaks, ragged rocks and lush forests, seems like an extension of the mighty and natural Hui Hill outside of the garden. The marvelous artificial hill in the garden and the two natural hills—Xi Hill and Hui Hill—outside the garden complement each other and merge into an integral whole. The beauty of the garden landscape is accented by the pleasant combination of the fantastic hill scenery and graceful water scenery.

The artificial hill is not only a visual treat, but also a tourist

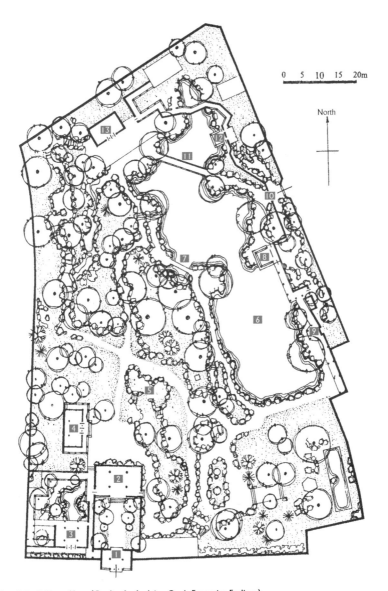

A Plan of the Ji Chang Yuan (Garden for Lodging One's Expansive Feelings)

The Ji Chang Yuan, which covers an area of about 10,000 square meters, is laid out by taking full advantage of its natural terrain, which is narrow from west to east and long from north to south. The artificial hill is built on the high land and the pond is dug on the low land. The scenes are built along the long central axis. By borrowing natural scenes from the Xi Hill and the Hui Hill, the Ji Chang Yuan boasts a hill-and-pond garden full of natural wonders.

1. Main Entrance 2. Shuangxiao Ancestral Temple 3. Bingli Hall 4. Hanzhen Study 5. Jiushi Terrace 6. Jinhuiyi Pond 7. Hebu Beach 8. Zhiyujian Pavilion 9. Yupan Pavilion 10. Qingxiang Moon Gate 11. Qixing Bridge 12. Hanbi Pavilion 13. Jiashu Hall

The Ji Chang Yuan

Far from being a big garden, the Ji Chang Yuan leaves behind in the mind of visitors a permanent impression that it is a deep, wide and spacious garden only because the designers are successful in borrowing scenes from outside the garden, which range from the nearby Zhu Hill to the Longguang Pagoda on the distant Xi Hill in the southeast. The borrowed scenes help to remove the visual restrictions for visitors. The Ji Chang Yuan is considered a successful example of adopting the technique of borrowing scenes in garden building.

attraction. Along the zigzag hill trail you can enjoy the unusual views of rare rocks. You will be attracted by the Bayin (which means "eight musical sounds") Creek which takes its source from the spring of the Hui Hill. The Bayin Creek is complete with a winding brook, a pond of limpid water, waterfalls and running spring, which combine to produce a melodious sound. The Bayin Creek is designed by leading the hidden spring water from outside the garden to the artificial hill through winding canals. The sound of the gurgling spring water as it flows down reverberates throughout the valley, thus creating a marvelous artistic ambience. Walking out of the Bayin Cave, you will reach the Jiushi (which means "nine lions") Terrace. It is a lofty mountain with a dense forest dotted with nine lion-shaped Taihu rocks.

As a well-designed compact garden that has produced marked results, the Ji Chang Yuan's reputation as a renowned garden in the south of the Yangtze River is well deserved.

11. He Yuan (He Garden)

The He Garden (also known as the Jixiao Mountain Villa), which is located in the Huayuan Street in the city of Yangzhou, Jiangsu Province, was built in the ninth year of the reign of Emperor Guangxu of the Qing dynasty. It is famed to be the biggest garden in Yangzhou.

The He Garden can be roughly divided into the eastern, central and western zones. The eastern zone used to be the residential quarters where the host entertained his guests. The South Residence was built against the wall. A four-facet hall stands to the north of the South Residence. The hall is the width of three rooms and is surrounded by a corridor. The ground outside the hall is paved with pebbles and tiles, which is patterned after rippled water. This stimulates the visitors' into imagining that the hall looks like a boat floating on the water. The residential quarters are separated from the central garden by a winding corridor. Visitors can glimpse the beautiful scenery of the central garden through the pane-free windows of various shapes on the corridor wall. This is another good example of obtaining a fine view by making full use of pane-free windows.

The principal landscape is concentrated in the central zone. Situated on the northern shoreline of the big expanse of the pond is a complex of seven buildings. With the middle three buildings standing higher than the rest and all the roof corners upturned, the architectural complex looks like a butterfly, hence the name "Butterfly Hall." Both floors of the hall are equipped with double-lane corridors that encircles the whole garden. The zigzag and meandering 400-plus-meter corridors are a great attraction to visitors. That section of double-lane corridor separating the central zone and the eastern zone serves as a partition of space. Meanwhile, the pane-free windows on the corridor wall links the scenery

The He Garden

In the middle of the pond in the central zone of the mountain villa is the Shuixin Pavilion. Sitting against the railing of the pavilion, visitors can observe the fish swimming in the pond or look at the beautiful surrounding architecture. If you come to the pavilion on a moonlit night, you are sure to have an unforgettable experience of seeing the reflection of the moon in the pond. The rock-piled crossing to its north and a zigzag flagstone bridge to its south are passageways leading to the northern and southern shore. The encircling double-lane corridor serves as the auditorium where visitors can enjoy performances.

between both zones. By making full use of those windows, visitors on either side can see the beautiful sights of both zones, thus expanding the respective garden space. This is a good example of taking full advantage of a corridor. The pond narrows down in the southwestern corner, and then expands into a bigger waterbody. Both shores of the north pond are decorated with artificial hills. The yellow stone cliff makes the hill look lofty and towering. The hill path built with Taihu rocks is full of twists and turns. The majestic artificial hills look like the product of Mother Nature.

The He Garden is characteristic of the vigorous and powerful style of gardens in Yangzhou. The landscape of the whole garden centers round the pond. The tracery walls and winding corridors produce layers upon layers of scenery. The connected halls, pavilions and artificial hills combine to create colorful scenes. The buildings and pavilions set off by rocks in the pond, and the meandering and zigzag double-lane corridors epitomize the characteristic style of local gardens.

12. Ge Yuan (Individual or Isolated Garden)

The Ge Yuan, which is located in the Dongguan Street (N) of Yangzhou, Jiangsu Province, was the private garden of Huang Yingtai, a salt merchant during the reign of Emperors Jiaqing and Daoguang of the Qing dynasty. It covers an area of about 11 acres.

As soon as you enter the garden, tall bamboos pleasing to both the eye and the mind will greet you. Against a background of the whitewashed wall, the bamboo grove is dotted with stalagmites of various shapes. It looks like a beautiful painting of the bamboo grove in spring. Behind the principal building—the Yiyu Hall—lies a pond with the reflections of the surrounding jagged rocks and ancient trees on the shore. Walking northward through the rock crossing, you will reach "Hutian-zichun," a seven-room building built along the wall. At the top of the building you can have a bird's-eye view of the whole garden. Walking eastward along the corridor of the building, you will reach an artificial hill built with yellow stones. The spiraling caves and trail lead you up and down. The changing cliffs and gullies, complemented by green ancient pine trees, look like a natural mountain. As it faces west, the hill glows golden during sunset. It is a simple painting of a forested mountain in autumn to contrast with the scene of the Yiyu Hall. At the southwestern hill of the autumn hill there is a small hall with a southern exposure called "toufeng-louyue." In front of the small hall stands a rockery of Xuan stones. Because the rockery is snow-white, it is called the "winter hill."

In China's gardens an artificial hill is regarded as a marvelous spectacle. There is a saying in the history of Chinese garden building: "Yangzhou is famous for its well-known gardens; and its gardens are

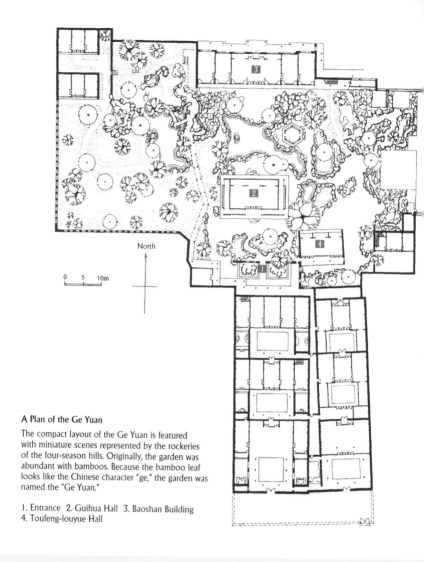

A Plan of the Ge Yuan

The compact layout of the Ge Yuan is featured with miniature scenes represented by the rockeries of the four-season hills. Originally, the garden was abundant with bamboos. Because the bamboo leaf looks like the Chinese character "ge," the garden was named the "Ge Yuan."

1. Entrance 2. Guihua Hall 3. Baoshan Building
4. Toufeng-louyue Hall

North

0 5 10m

famous for their artificial hills." The uncanny craftsmanship of the artificial hills of the Ge Yuan named after the four seasons are beyond description. Its polished stalagmites distinguish the spring hill. The summer hill is known for its rocks and caves. The autumn hill overlooks a beautiful distant view. The winter hill seems to be blanketed with melting snow. All of them are typical of Yangzhou-style artificial hills.

The Ge Yuan

The Yiyu Hall–the principal building of the garden, which is open on four sides–is also known as the Guihua (which means "osmanthus") Hall, because the courtyard in front is planted with fragrant osmanthus. There is a lake-like pond behind the hall. With outstretched arms, branches and brooks, the waterbody is seemingly fluid and natural.

The Summer Hill of the Ge Yuan

There is a pond to the southwest of the Hutian-zichun Building. The artificial hill built with Taihu rocks on the northern shore of the pond is composed of winding brooks, curved shoreline, secluded caves and stalactites shaded by a lush forest. There are deep, cool and secluded caves inside the hill. The outside is covered with lush shaded trees. As the scene is typical of summer time, the hill is thus called "summer hill."

13. Yu Yuan (Garden to Please)

The Yu Yuan, which is located near the Town God's Temple, is one of the famous classical gardens in Shanghai. Its construction started in 1559 and was completed in 1577. After entering the main entrance, you will be greeted by the gorgeously high Sansui (which means "three ears of grain") Hall. The hall was used as a place for public gatherings. It is elegantly decorated with the carvings of ears of rice, melons and other fruits to symbolize the celebration of a good harvest, thus giving its name of "Sansui Hall."

The Yangshan Hall and the Juanyu Building behind the Sansui Hall are eye-catching with delicate upturned eaves and a brilliant red railing.

Starting from the artificial hill, the Jianru-jiajing Winding Corridor leads to the courtyard in the east which houses the Wanhua Tower, the Yule Pavilion and the Huixin-buyuan Pavilion. The pond in front of the Wanhua Tower is connected with the lake water under the Grand Artificial Hill. With the whitewashed wall as an excellent backdrop, the limpid creek flows in a zigzag way and passes the Moon Gate, which gives visitors an impression that this is a perpetual stream. You can see in front of the Wanhua Tower the ginkgo tree that was planted in the Ming dynasty and the magnolia tree covered with thick foliage. To the east of the hall is an architectural complex centered around the Dianchun Hall. The Acting and Singing Stage is located in front of the Dianchun Hall and several houses stand against the wall to its east. A brook is running through a cave underneath.

Walking southward from the Dianchun Hall, you will find yourself in the Yulinglong Scenic Spot. A huge natural rock called "Yulinglong" towers above the front of the Yuhua Hall. With a height of three-plus

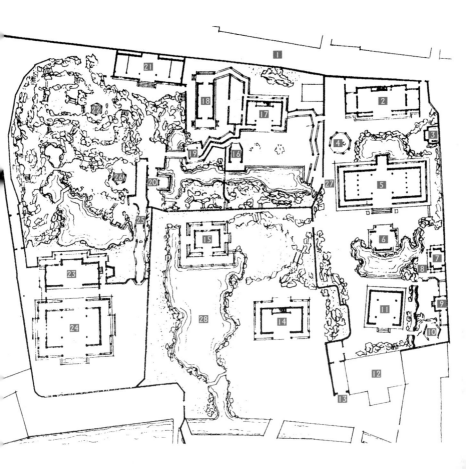

A General Plan of the Yu Yuan

Pan En, the original owner of the Yu Yuan, was a minister during the reign of Emperor Jiajing of the Ming dynasty. He built this garden for the purpose of pleasing his parents, which is why he named it "Yu (which literally means 'to please') Yuan." The original garden covered an area of about 70 *mu*. During the late period of the Ming dynasty the Yu Yuan had several different owners and it was divided into two parts—eastern part and western part. The present-day Yu Yuan is a section in the northeastern part of the original garden. It covers an area of only about 30 *mu*.

1. Fuyou Road 2. Depository of Treasures, Qinghuo Room (upstairs) 3. Xuepu Veranda 4. Well Pavilion 5. Dianchun Hall 6. Fengwu-yingming Acting and Singing Stage 7. Kuai Tower 8. Baoyun Rock 9. Jingyi Veranda 10. Tingli Pavilion 11. Hexi Hall 12. Master Lao Hall 13. Dianchun Hall 14. Deyi Building 15. Jiushi Study 16. Liangyi Veranda 17. Wanhua Tower 18. Yifang Boat-shaped Hall 19. Square Pavilion 20. Yule Pavilion 21. Cuixiu Hall 22. Wangjiang Pavilion 23. Juanyushu Chamber (upstairs), Yangshan Hall (downstairs) 24. Sansui Hall 25. Jianru-jiajing Winding Corridor 26. Yixiu Pavilion 27. Chuanyun Pavilion 28. Pond

The Yu Yuan

The Sansui Hall faces the pond. The yellow-stone Grand Artificial Hill across the pond looks vigorous and imposing. The hill is lush with flowers and trees and crisscrossed by narrow trails. The reflections of the hill, pavilions and towers in the pond present a picturesque scene.

meters, the rock is delicately shaped and ingeniously made. This rock is the comprehensive manifestation of all the unique features of the Taihu rock, i.e., wrinkled, penetrating, leaky, slim and delicate. Legend has it that this rock was left behind from the flotilla of rare flowers and rocks collected in the south of the Yangtze River that was shipping to Emperor Huizong of the Song dynasty. This rock has become one of the most famous works of art among the rocks collected in the south of the Yangtze River.

Overlooking to the southern direction from the Dianchun Hall, you'll catch sight of an inner courtyard complete with halls, pavilions and towers in a refined architectural style. It looks exactly like a garden within a garden.

14. Xiao Pan Gu (Xiaopangu Garden)

The Xiaopangu Garden, which is located on Dashu Street in the southeast of Yangzhou's new city, covers an area of about 0.3 hectare.

After you enter the garden by passing a moon gate on one side of the main hall, you'll find yourself in a small courtyard with three drawing rooms in its northern part. Turning the eastern corner of the flower hall and walking northward, you'll be greeted by the beautiful scenery complete with hills, rockeries and ponds. The zigzag layout of the Hua Hall faces the hills and ponds in the northeast. To the north of the Hua Hall is a lakeside pavilion connected with a winding corridor along the wall. The pavilion, which adds to the beauty of the Flowery Hall and the Grand Artificial Hill, built with Taihu rocks face each other across the pond. A zigzag bridge divides the well-laid-out moderate pond into two parts, thus increasing the gradation and depth of the water scenery and creating a pond mouth. After crossing the zigzag bridge, you will reach the entrance to the cave of the Grand Artificial Hill on the eastern shoreline. The wide and secluded cave is furnished with chess tables and stools. Visitors can relax and enjoy the cool breeze, play chess or chat. The daylight streams into the cave through the holes on the cave wall. The exit of the cave is located near the pond. In order to get to the drawing room at the northern end of the garden, visitors can climb the stone steps or take the rock walkway to cross the pond. The zigzag stone steps in front of the drawing room will lead you to the top of the Grand Artificial Hill. You can climb up the mountain from there through the valley-like path called "shuiliu-yunzai."

Local people call the Grand Artificial Hill "Jiushitu (which means 'a painting of nine lions') Hill." This is one of the masterpieces in rockery

The Xiaopangu Garden

Though a small garden, the Xiaopangu Garden is distinguished by the sparse use of land, the differential arrangement of space and variation between obstruction and transparency. The rockeries and buildings, which are concentrated on both shorelines of the pond, face each other across the pond in an attractive way. Peaks, stone walls, gorges and stone steps are complemented by flowers and trees as well as the simple and graceful halls, pavilions and corridors. The harmonious combination of natural landscape and man-made buildings demonstrates the elegant and refined style of gardens in the south of the Yangtze River.

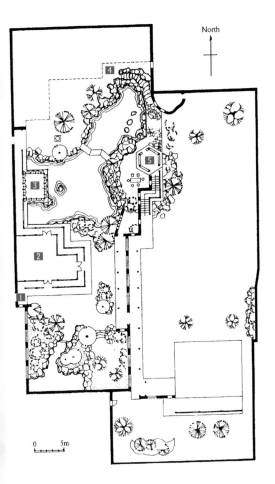

A Plan of the Xiaopangu Garden

As a small residential garden, the Xiaopangu Garden was first built during the reign of Emperor Qianlong of the Qing dynasty. Zhou Fu, Governor-general of Guangdong and Guangxi owned it during the reign of Emperor Guangxu of the Qing dynasty. Today, only the western part of the original garden is kept intact while the rest of it has long fallen into disuse.

1. Entrance 2. Flowery Hall 3. Lakeside Pavilion 4. Shuiliu-yunzai Climbing Path 5. Feng Pavilion

building in the Jiangnan (which means "south of the Yangtze River") style. The main body of the hill is built with Taihu rocks. On one side of the pavilion is a towering peak, which stands 9 meters above the water surface that looks vivid and natural. The curved shoreline wall is also built with Taihu rocks. The deliberately dotted holes on the shoreline wall are meant to give visitors the impression that it is the result of constant erosion. This is a Yangzhou-style technique commonly adopted in building the stone wall of an embankment.

15. Gong Wang Fu (Prince Gong's Mansion)

Located in Shishahai district in central Beijing, the Cuijin Garden is also known as the back garden of the Prince Gong's Mansion. The original garden was built in the Ming dynasty. With an area of 2.7 hectares, the garden is divided into three tourist routes, i.e., the central, eastern and western routes. The central route is symmetrical in its layout and the north-south axis is identical to the central axis of the mansion. The central route includes the entrance and three rows of residential compounds.

The layout of the eastern and western routes is flexible and unrestricted. The eastern route is focused on closely spaced buildings, which mainly consists of three compounds of different architectural styles. The western route is centered on the pond. The rectangular pond is known for the stone wall of its embankment and the fish watching terrace. Open Hall on the islet in the pond. Its western and southern shores each have an earth hill. A winding corridor separates the eastern shore. The landscaped buildings on the northern shoreline form an independent scenic spot with emphasis on water scenery.

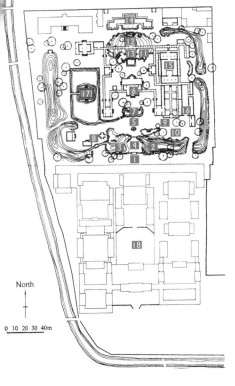

The Cuijin Garden of Gong Wang Fu

As a garden attached to the Gong Wang Fu, the Cuijin Garden is characteristic of an imperial garden. The overall layout is a harmonious combination of the beauty of a landscaped garden and the solemn and impressive bearing of a royal family. The color and decoration of the buildings are more gaudy and resplendent than those of the private gardens in northern China. The rockeries are built with both Pianyun grey stones and Taihu rocks in the bold and vigorous northern style. Ancient trees, weeping willows, colorful flowers, tall bamboos and dense vines also distinguish the garden.

A Plan of the Gong Wang Fu

The Cuijin Garden lies next to the Prince Gong's Mansion. By tracing the origin of the ancient trees and rockeries in the garden, we guess that the original garden was probably built in the Ming dynasty and it was renovated in the Qing dynasty.

1. Entrance 2. Chuiqingyue Chinese Scholartrees 3. Cuiyun Hill 4. Qujing-tongyou Path 5. Feilai Rock 6. Anshan Hall 7. Fu River 8. Yuguan Pass 9. Qinqiu Pavilion 10. Yishu Garden 11. Dicui Rockery 12. Lütian-xiaoyin Hall 13. Yaoyue Terrace 14. Fu Hall 15. Grand Theatre 16. Yinxiang-zuiyue Gate 17. Guanyutai Hall 18. Prince Gong's Mansion

North

0 10 20 30 40m

111

16. Tui Si Yuan
(Retreat & Reflection Garden)

Located in Tongli Township of Wujiang, Jiangsu Province, the Retreat & Reflection Garden is about 11 miles away from Suzhou.

The sparse layout of the garden is well planned. The garden is composed of the residential quarters on the left, central halls in the middle and a garden on the right. The halls and courtyards serve as a link between the residential area and the garden. The principal building "Tui Si Residence" is situated in the northern part of the garden. The moon gazing platform lies in front of the residence overlooking the rippled pond. To the west of the residence stands the Shuixiangxie Pavilion. A music room is hidden at the end of the pond to its east. The Tui Si Residence, the Shuixiangxie Pavilion and the music room combine to form the landscape of the northern part of the garden. A winding corridor connects all the important scenic spots. Visitors can enjoy constantly changing scenes while walking along the corridor.

By crossing caves and climbing stone steps, visitors can reach the Overhead Bridge linking the Xintai Building and the Guyu-shengliang Chamber. The overpass-like constructing technique is seldom used in garden building.

The Tui Si Yuan (Retreat & Reflection Garden)

Visitors enter the garden by passing the central halls and a moon gate. The zigzag corridor leads them to the scenes in the garden. The layout of the garden centers on the pond. The moderate pond looks pleasing to the eye with its curved shoreline decorated with rockeries, flowers and trees. The principal buildings around the pond are so close to the water that the garden is also known as a "close-to-water garden."

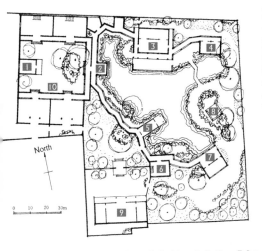

North

0 10 20 30m

A Plan of the Tui Si Yuan (Retreat & Reflection Garden)

Tongli is a famous township with a long history situated in the region of rivers and lakes in the south of the Yangtze River. Every household in Tongli is accessible by boat. With convenient water and land transport, the township is economically prosperous and culturally advanced. It became a favorable place of residence for many eminent families living in different dynasties. As a result, there are more than 30 garden-attached mansions. Ren Lansheng built the Retreat & Reflection Garden after he resigned from his post as a provincial official of Anhui during the reign of Emperor Guangxu of the Qing dynasty and returned to his hometown. He named the garden "Retreat and Reflection Garden" to express the sentiment that he should reflect on his faults after he retired from public life. The Retreat & Reflection Garden became one of the famous private gardens in the south of the Yangtze River.

1. Boat-shaped Waterside House 2. Shuixiangxie Pavilion 3. Retreat & Reflection Residence 4. Music Room
5. Naohong-yige Stone Boat 6. Xintai Building 7. Guyu-shengliang Chamber 8. Mianyun Pavilion 9. Guihua Hall 9. Central Halls

17. Yu Yin Shan Fang (Mountain Cottage of Abundant Shade)

Located in Nancun Township in the Panyu District of Guangzhou, Guangdong Province, the Yu Yin Shan Fang is one of the four famous gardens in Lingnan (a geographic area referring to lands in the south of China's Five Ranges, situated at the border area of Guangdong, Guangxi and Jiangxi provinces). The garden, which was first built during the reign of Emperor Tongzhi of the Qing dynasty, is still in good condition.

The architectural style of the Yu Yin Shan Fang embodies the blend of Chinese and Western cultures. Its overall layout is spectacular. The ponds are built in the European practical style. A square pond and a round pond constitute the water scenery. The buildings of the Yu Yin Shan Fang are built in an open style with colorful carvings, such as elegant wood carving, brick carving and plaster sculpture. The wooden beams of the principal buildings are carved with various themed patterns: one hundred animals, one hundred children, one hundred birds paying homage to the phoenix, etc. Some accessorial decorations, such as railing and carved designs, are done in the European garden-building style. This offers a good example of the combination of Chinese and Western styles. As Guangzhou is situated in the subtropical zone, the Yu Yin Shan Fang is distinguished by its evergreen trees and fully blossomed flowers all year round.

The Yu Yin Shan Fang

The western part is centered on the square pond. The Linchi-bieguan Study on the southern shore and the Shenliu Hall (the main hall) on the northern shore face each other across the pond, constituting a north-south central axis of the western zone. There is a corridor on the eastern shore and an arch bridge with a pavilion on it in the middle. The horizontal axis formed by the arch bridge and the square pond crosses the north-south central axis at the center of the pond. Stretching eastward, the horizontal axis will meet the axis of the principal building "Linglong-shuixie Pavilion" in the eastern part of the garden, thus forming the west-east axis of the whole garden.

A Plan of the Yu Yin Shan Fang (Mountain Cottage of Abundant Shade)

After you enter the garden through a gate in the southwestern corner, you'll come to a small courtyard. On its western side a wintersweet is planted against the wall, thus forming a miniature scene. Passing the moon gate on the right, you'll be faced with a wall sculpture. Walking northward, you'll reach the second gate. The couplet hung on the gate implies the name of the garden. Crossing the gate, you will find yourself in the western part of the garden.

1. Entrance 2. Linchi-bieguan Study 3. Shenliu Hall 4. Lanhe Hall 5. Linglong-shuixie Pavilion 6. Nanxun Pavilion 7. Boat-shaped Hall 8. Study 9. Ancestral Hall

APPENDICES

Translation of Garden Names Accessible to Visitors

English Name	Pinyin	Chinese Character	Location
Ancient Garden of Elegance	Gu Yi Yuan	古猗园	Shanghai
Beihai Park	Bei Hai Gong Yuan	北海公园	Beijing
Blue Waves Pavilion	Cang Lang Ting	沧浪亭	Suzhou, Jiangsu Province
Chengde Mountain Resort	Bi Shu Shan Zhuang	避暑山庄	Chengde, Hebei Province
Garden for Lodging One's Expansive Feelings	Ji Chang Yuan	寄畅园	Wuxi, Jiangsu Province
Garden of Arts	Yi Pu	艺圃	Suzhou, Jiangsu Province
Garden of Autumn Vapours	Qiu Xia Pu	秋霞圃	Shanghai
Garden to Please	Yu Yuan	豫园	Shanghai
He Garden	He Yuan	何园	Yangzhou, Jiangsu Province
Humble Administrator's Garden	Zhuo Zheng Yuan	拙政园	Suzhou, Jiangsu Province
Individual or Isolated Garden	Ge Yuan	个园	Yangzhou, Jiangsu Province
Lingering Garden	Liu Yuan	留园	Suzhou, Jiangsu Province
Lion Grove	Shi Zi Lin	狮子林	Suzhou, Jiangsu Province
Master of thr Nets Garden	Wang Shi Yuan	网师园	Suzhou, Jiangsu Province
Mountain Cottage of Abundant Shade	Yu Yin Shan Fang	余荫山房	Guangzhou, Guangdong Province
Mountain Villa Surounded by Flourishing Greenery	Huan Xiu Shan Zhuang	环秀山庄	Suzhou, Jiangsu Province
Old Summer Palace	Yuan Ming Yuan	圆明园	Beijing
Outlook Garden	Zhan Yuan	瞻园	Nanjing, Jiangsu Province
Prince Gong's Mansion	Gong Wang Fu	恭王府	Beijing
Retreat & Reflction Garden	Tui Si Yuan	退思园	Wujiang, Jiangsu Province
Silver of Rock Mountain Cottage	Pian Shi Shan Fang	片石山房	Yangzhou, Jiangsu Province
Slender West Lake	Shou Xi Hu	瘦西湖	Yangzhou, Jiangsu Province
Summer Palace	Yi He Yuan	颐和园	Beijing
Warm Garden	Xu Yuan	煦园	Nanjing, Jiangsu Province
Xiaopangu Garden	Xiao Pan Gu	小盘谷	Yangzhou, Jiangsu Province

Dynasties in Chinese History

Xia Dynasty	2070 BC – 1600 BC
Shang Dynasty	1600 BC – 1046 BC
Zhou Dynasty	1046 BC – 256 BC
Western Zhou Dynasty	1046 BC – 771 BC
Eastern Zhou Dynasty	770 BC – 256 BC
Spring and Autumn Period	770 BC – 476 BC
Warring States Period	475 BC – 221 BC
Qin Dynasty	221 BC – 206 BC
Han Dynasty	206 BC – 220 AD
Western Han Dynasty	206 BC – 25 AD
Eastern Han Dynasty	25 – 220
Three Kingdoms	220 – 280
Wei	220 – 265
Shu Han	221 – 263
Wu	222 – 280
Jin Dynasty	265 – 420
Western Jin Dynasty	265 – 316
Eastern Jin Dynasty	317 – 420
Northern and Southern Dynasties	420 – 589
Southern Dynasties	420 – 589
Northern Dynasties	439 – 581
Sui Dynasty	581 – 618
Tang Dynasty	618 – 907
Five Dynasties and Ten States	907 – 960
Five Dynasties	907 – 960
Ten States	902 – 979
Song Dynasty	960 – 1279
Northern Song Dynasty	960 – 1127
Southern Song Dynasty	1127 – 1279
Liao Dynasty	916 – 1125
Jin Dynasty	1115 – 1234
Xixia Dynasty	1038 – 1227
Yuan Dynasty	1279 – 1368
Ming Dynasty	1368 – 1644
Qing Dynasty	1644 – 1911